When Doves Cry

David V. Hunt

Copyright © 2016 David V. Hunt

All rights reserved.

ISBN-13: 978-0692769171

VULNERABILITY

Vulnerability challenges us to confront our fears. It creates bonds between others as we open up and encourages others to open up. Typically, we view vulnerability as a weakness; we feel unprotected, naked, and exposed to criticism and judgment. Quite the contrary; vulnerability sets us on the path of solving some of our greatest challenges. Our ability to articulate some significant fear or insecurity makes us more human, more able to connect. Being vulnerable pulls truth, honesty, and understanding from our lives. We embrace and engage with others stories. In this book, I've placed my insecurities, challenges, and fears in hopes of connecting on a deeper level with people and in some way bringing more value to your life. I hope you enjoy.

CONTENTS

	Acknowledgments	i
	Preface & Introduction	1

Section I

1	Informing Our Existence	7
2	The Inadequacy Of Self	10
3	The Present: Pt. I	15
4	The Present: Pt. II	30
5	The Future	32
6	Hakuna Matata	36
7	The Gratitude Paradox	44
8	Acknowledging Our Existence	59
9	Self-Discovery	68

Section II

10	Earthquake	84
11	Epicenter, Magnitude, & Focus	113

Section III

12	The Framework	130
13	The Matthew Story	139

ACKNOWLEDGMENTS

The Purple One

PREFACE & INTRODUCTION

Preface

On May 16, 1984, Prince released the song *When Doves Cry*. It was a profound piece of work, which received critical acclaim and numerous accolades. It was beautiful, but its very beauty was rooted in anguish and pain. The song characterized the history of a child who had experienced trauma in his youth, a struggle that was translated into a groundbreaking piece of music. When Doves Cry was emblematic of the experiences so many of us have with our history and the results those experiences have on our lives in future generations. Understanding those results can only be achieved through careful consideration of the past.

We don't have to the perpetuate struggles and challenges that have brought themselves into existence under the radar of our own awareness. We can excel beyond the cycles that challenge our lives and break free from the bonds that stifle our independence. Maybe you are like your father. Maybe you are like your mother. Maybe you're just like your cousin, sister, or brother. But that does not have to be your reality if you don't want it to be and more importantly, if it isn't beneficial to you. This book is about happiness. It is about creating the happiness we desire by considering the implications of our past and understanding ourselves. This is what it sounds like when doves...dance, smile, become happy, you decide.

Introduction

From an outside view, your life may look great. The truth, however, is that people probably don't know that you're struggling at your job, you can't pay your rent, or are having marital problems. You go through life hiding your problems away from the world, repressing them and finding ways to keep pushing along. No matter how much you try, the problems don't stop; they keep popping up. This book isn't for the people whose lives are completely wonderful. This is for the people who are facing some struggle, the ones who don't have it all figured out. This was written for the people who can at least attempt to be real with themselves and honest about moving towards progress.

This was very much the case for me as I entered my senior year of college. Life was at a standstill; I was twelve thousand dollars in credit card debt; the vast majority of which came from many drunken nights, I didn't have a way to pay for a thirty-thousand dollar tuition bill, I was going through the fifth breakup with my girlfriend of three years, my dad was about to lose his house, one of his cars had already been repossessed, and his business was failing to the tune of a two-hundred thousand dollar debt load. I constantly struggled to pay my rent on time and my bank account was in overdraft every few months. I had racked up an eighteen-hundred dollar utility bill forcing my gas at my apartment to be shut off. With no heat, I took cold showers and used frozen dinners that I could microwave with my still available electricity.

My relationship with both of my parents was in rapid decline, to the point that I stopped visiting home or talking to them as much because I would get so annoyed with them. To compensate, I was constantly partying on the weekends and spending money that I didn't have while drinking unhealthy amounts of alcohol, harming both my health and my social life. I was failing at life and I really couldn't conceive of a way to escape it all.

I started to try and understand why I was experiencing so much shit. Life sucked. I mean it really sucked, but I knew I didn't have anyone to blame except for myself. To be honest, considering my life as a bad one was very rare. Typically, I was an extremely happy person with great purpose in life. We can all lose our way sometimes. It seemed like everything just got topsy turvy out of nowhere. Deep inside though, I knew that where I was, was the consequence of my own actions. However, I could not for the life of me figure how to escape from it all. When I actually gave my problems some real thought, I came to realize that it wasn't the first time I had experienced them before. In some way, they were similar to others that I had faced and it was apparent that my problems were repeating themselves. They had the same fundamental qualities, which led me to believe that I had to be consistently doing something wrong if I kept experiencing them.

I started to question my most challenging problems. Where had they come from, why was I facing them, and what could I do to get rid of them? What I came to understand about my own problems had significant implications for other people's lives as well. I wasn't alone. Other people faced problems in their lives that seemed to repeat themselves too. Often times these repetitive problems are the most significant ones we face. Tense relationships with our parents, an inability to connect with our children, poor friendships, unsatisfying and unfulfilling jobs, personal insecurities, anger management issues; the list goes on. But it feels like we never manage to get over the constant barrage of problems that we face. Inevitably, we end up facing those challenges over and over again because we never understood the underlying reasons why we experienced them in the first place. No one ever taught us how to break the cycle; to question our past experiences, identify similarities between problems, and make a change. As a result, we continued with our traditional approach to living, perpetuating our traditional problems and compounding their traditional effects on our lives.

It was time for a change. So I began an intense self-study, trying to identify the origins of my most significant challenges. Questioning where I learned certain behaviors from and the impacts they were having on my life. I started to realize that understanding how to break the cycles of my problems was much simpler than I originally thought it would be. I initially expected that correcting the challenges I faced would be a long and drawn out process that required too much energy. Contrary to that belief, I found that by asking myself a set of very specific questions, I was to able completely transform how I had historically approached my problems and create more happiness in my life. Those questions became the foundation for creating a process to identify and break the problematic cycles that I faced in my life.

The simplicity of the process encouraged me to consider if it could be applied to the lives of others. If it held the benefit of breaking down my own problematic barriers that existed for so long, and in such a short time, could it do the same for other people? Through much iteration by means of studying people's individual histories, I found the process to be widely applicable. By using it, people could gain an understanding for the origin of their own problematic cycles and create ways to break them. Maybe we think our problems are too complex. Maybe we don't think we actually have problems. Perhaps, we are simply used to our challenges and have been able to ignore them. Despite whatever it may be that keeps our problems prominent in our lives, questioning the origins of our behaviors has many benefits for overcoming them.

My initial thoughts in writing this book were to consider what the implications of those questions might be. Can they really help us see why we face certain challenges in our lives? Could they give us insight into how we could overcome our most challenging problems? Would they possibly, be able to even help us predict what type of challenges we may face in the future? Ultimately, I was seeking to understand that if questioning the origins of our tendencies could inform us of the origins of our problems, how could we break that repetition and as a result, experience greater levels of happiness?

An underlying assumption when approaching these questions was that we form a substantial amount of our beliefs about people, relationships, and events very early on in life. Those experiences were in large part responsible for shaping how we came to react to the situations that we ultimately faced. My suspicion was that not many of us choose to question those experiences. We may not fully understand the role they play in either helping or hurting our lives. For example, the learning a son or daughter would gain from parents who have been married for fifty years and always seemed to be in love has a strong impact on their own intimate relationships. However, if that same couple always had fleeting friendships, the results for that son or daughter's relationships with their friends may be a bit more challenging.

As I examined the experiences of others, I began to notice very specific similarities that enabled me to create a process for understanding problems and creating solutions for them. The reason that some of our most significant problems cycle in and out of our lives is fundamentally rooted in our past experiences. Most of the time, we don't recognize that our problems exist in this way. When we take a more involved look into our personal histories, we can examine why we constantly face limitations on our growth and overall dissatisfaction with life. This eliminates the need to, as we so often do, react to our overwhelming problems by quickly changing our actions. By doing this, we never realize something more fundamental: that we are stifled by our thought processes and will experience more trouble growing if we don't learn to reflect *and* change them. While the answers to our problems may be found through our past, the ability to overcome them exists right now.

This is a book about happiness. It is about creating the happiness we want by considering the implications of our past. The information that our previous experiences hold is substantial. We never know who we truly are and why we face certain challenges and opportunities until we gain an understanding of where we have come from. This book isn't about justifying our problems, it is about understanding them. It is about tracing their origin from past experiences and creating a more joy-filled life. Why am I the way I am? What did my parents do that I still do today? What problems of my past are still challenging me right now? The traits that we pick up; our voice intonation, physical mannerisms, and responses to various stimuli have each been taught to some extent. Understanding which experiences taught them and if they remain valuable to us today is paramount to our happiness.

When I wrote this introduction, I started to consider the happiness that this understanding had created in my life and potentially could for others. While writing, I was sitting on a train heading home from work. A woman directly across from me was reading *The Bell Jar* by Sylvia Plath. Her legs are crossed and her face is buried in her book. I wonder where she learned that reading posture from. The train comes to a stop and a young man is standing waiting for the doors to open. He is braced forward as if the train were still moving. One woman, towards the back checks her phone with one hand while the other hand twirls her hair. I wonder where they learned these mannerisms from. I wonder what problems they might be experiencing and if they too can break the cycles by considering their origin.

> How can u just leave me standing?
> Alone in a world that's so cold?
> Maybe I'm just 2 demanding
> Maybe I'm just like my father, 2 bold
> Maybe I'm just like my mother
> She's never satisfied
> Why do we scream at each other?
> This is what it sounds like
> When doves cry
>
>   - Prince

1 | INFORMING OUR EXISTENCE

Learning from the Past

"Progress, far from consisting in change, depends on retentiveness. When change is absolute there remains no being to improve and no direction is set for possible improvement: and when experience is not retained, as among savages, infancy is perpetual. Those who cannot remember the past are condemned to repeat it."

– George Santayana

When we do not learn from our experiences, we do not grow. We can never substantially improve or expand beyond our circumstances. That is a huge challenge to face: feeling like life is always against us or that we can't escape. We find ourselves losing clarity and total control of our lives. Always fighting to make it through to another day because our problems are pressing down on us like heavy weights. It seems like so much is against us, and even if we see the bright side, there is always a shadow of our problems that sticks out. Problems are not to be trifled with; they are serious things. Particularly, the problems that continue to face us on a seemingly repetitive basis are the ones that we should give the most attention. Not to blow them out of proportion but to understand how we can change them.

As infants, we lived very carefree lives. For the most part, someone was always there to take care of us, we always got what we wanted: be it food, milk, or toys, and if we didn't; we would cry to get them. Tears became the currency of our infancy - they are what we learned our parents would exchange for almost anything. The beautiful thing about crying was that it was intuitive and it was an unlimited resource. No one taught us how to cry but we certainly knew that if we did it, we could get anything we wanted: a juice bottle, another bedtime story, a glass of milk, or a lullaby.

As we grew older, however, rules because the basic framework of our lives and our crying currency was devalued. We couldn't go outside after a certain time, we had to do our homework, go to school; rules upon rules upon rules! For many of them, we initially tried to respond the way we always had; we threw a tantrum. We'd cry and scream and become increasingly vocal about these new limits that were imposed on our lives. However, we soon realized that these tactics would no longer work, at least not as successfully. What was once crying and wailing our arms in the air was responded to with reprimand. A tap on the tush, a verbal warning, or other forms of punishment began to ensue. Pretty soon, we learned that a tantrum was not the way to get that toy we wanted or to go and play with our friends. We had to suck it up, do our chores, or worse, eat our vegetables. To find out that we had to do something other than simply get upset and cry required us to somehow reflect on our past experiences. They became the foundation for understanding what was appropriate in the future. Without that reflection, which back then seemed natural, we would have continued to pout and throw tantrums, all to no avail.

While this may seem a bit simplistic, the same is true today and it conveys a very important fact. That from infancy, we have used our past experiences to mold our approach towards life. This includes how we react to situations, who we decide to interact with, how we spend the majority of our time, and more. While these characteristics may have been easily embedded into our psyche when we were younger, somewhere along the way, we became more selective in our reflection processes. We put up barriers to only take in the information that we wanted, regardless of if it was valuable or not. For many of us, we began to discriminate against some of the most important information; the information about ourselves.

Blaming our environment for the problems that we face instead of fully acknowledging our role in the challenges we experience. Criticizing others as a way to compensate for some insecurity that we may have. Using things like drugs, alcohol, sex, or even food to hide away from the truth of having to face ourselves. It makes sense though; those things feel good. They feel a lot better than facing our problems or reflecting and being honest with ourselves. Inevitably, those actions become dependencies and they desensitize us to the problems we are really facing. They never actually solve anything, they just increase an ultimately negative effect. This happens because we don't expose ourselves to enough of our own lives, of our own past experiences. This phenomenon has been an extremely detrimental epidemic that has plagued society for many years. We don't know why we hate the things we hate and why we love the things we love. We never know why we are so adamant about certain beliefs without ever questioning them. We never know why we are afraid of dogs but love cats. Why we can't stand the zoo or hate being outdoors. We never understand why we are, the way we are. And without that information, what can we expect? Just more of the same.

When we begin to expose ourselves to more information about our own personal histories, we begin the reflection process which is the foundation for breaking the continuous problems we face. It is not until we can ask ourselves the questions about our past that we are afraid of that we can escape the self-perpetuating cycles of our life's problems that have stifled us. And even though that is just the first step, it is an extremely important first step. We have to use this knowledge to expand ourselves beyond our situations and grow. If we want to experience better lives; it is in more than just our hands, it is in our histories.

A better life is not the result of harder work, longer hours, more discipline, or more money. A better and more fulfilling life is the result of understanding the *why* of your existence and that begins with questioning your past. That takes a great degree of confidence and patience, because questioning our past isn't necessarily the modus operandi of society. While we have been exposed to many things: the aspects of our lives at present and our aspirations of the future, our past has not been high on the priority list.

2 | THE INADEQUACY OF SELF

We have not been appropriately informed of our existence. We have been stifled by society and desensitized to our own intricate lives. With massive amounts of distractions preventing us from even the desire to question ourselves, it is no wonder that we run into challenges in our lives. Our world doesn't place a high priority on the past. While many historical occurrences are documented they aren't questioned for their future implications. The media shows us the material sides of who and what we want to become but ignores the greatness of who we are. The lists can go on; ranging from entertainment icons screaming "Yolo" and advocating a life of erratic behaviors to an over-preoccupation of 'what's next' for our careers.

We are never satisfied, and rightly so: we should never be. But we should also remember that these extremes in information can inhibit our happiness. Listening too much to what is *right now* or what *can be* the future blinds us to understanding how important the past actually is and the impact it has had on who we are and who we are becoming. The opposite is also true when we spend too much time dwelling on the past and missing out on life. The focus of modern society has been too extreme and actually ends up creating more problems. Nothing encourages us to place all of that into context, however. We are constantly looking at where we are and seeing that we haven't reached where we want to be. That emphasis creates the perception of being inadequate, which can be demoralizing and depressive.

We begin to think about our failures without proper attention on our successes. Balanced attention should be given towards where we are, where we want to be, and also where we have been. Without the correct understanding of the relationship between all three, we may continue to grow but the problems that haunt us now will stifle us in the future, if they are not already. No one should feel as if they aren't worth it, like they don't deserve happiness, or like they are just plain inadequate. That is a very dark place to be in. When we get there, escaping it can be harder than anything we've ever encountered before.

I used to have a very close friend, Sophia. She faced these feelings of inadequacy more than any other person that I have known. When she went off to college, Sophia began to experience one intimate relationship after another, each failing far worse than the preceding one. In the face of these failures, she would constantly feel like she wasn't good enough. Sophia spiraled down into a deep depression; feeling challenged by what was going wrong and what she couldn't change. The stress on her mind had physical effects and she struggled to maintain the will to move on. But even amid the constant men in her life who took advantage of this; she remained resilient. Her relationships would ebb and flow, with men initially swooping in like a savior from her problems from a previous relationship and then when the relationship would get tense; back out, becoming verbally or physically abusive.

They would cast constant criticism on her, so much so that Sophia internalized that criticism and it ultimately became her own view of herself. She was hurting and she thought of herself as a horrible person. She couldn't keep a relationship, faced critiques by multiple people, and couldn't seem to find anyone to love her for who she was. So she spent her time considering those facts of the present moment and blaming herself for her past actions. Sophia didn't think to her future; she was too caught up in the troubles of what was currently happening in her life. In consideration of the past and the present, it was to place fault on herself and how she had ruined her relationships. She never fully acknowledged the role that two people played in a relationship- how could she? She faced constant attacks from her suitors about how she wasn't good enough. But why? Why did she keep doing this amid friends telling her how amazing she was and numerous accolades telling her how smart she was? Scholarships telling her how successful she was going to be? None of that mattered; her energy was consumed in her failures of her relationships, but why?

These experiences that Sophia was going through were striking because for most of our friendship, she had been a very driven, ambitious, and determined person. Her love of art extended from the canvas to the kitchen. She didn't seek approval from anyone except herself and she didn't let a lot of things get in her way. Sophia was extremely bright, highly motivated, and very active in community oriented projects. Not to mention, she was gorgeous as hell. So to see her troubled by these relationships was shaking. And to see the sustained effect they had on her life and her perspective towards life was incomprehensible. There was a corollary to it all, however, which was her mother and father's relationship. They had separated when Sophia and her sister were younger, leaving a very strong impression on their memories. It was a rough separation and one that their mother took to heart. While Sophia's mother struggled to reconcile the relationship, her father maintained control. He criticized her and made it known that they were not to be together, however, Sophia's mother could never let go. Even through the constant barrage of critiques, she would be there for him. If he wanted her, he could have her.

The same was true for Sophia. Both Sophia and her mother were heavily mistreated by men. They were never able to fall out of love and as a result of the stresses, they experienced tremendous health challenges. They were unable to let go of someone who was, from the outside very clearly wrong for them. That is embedded in Sophia. She learned from her mother how to approach relationships. Ultimately, she falls for the same type of men who will exploit her weaknesses because she has no gauge for what a good man is or should be. The most influential exposure to relationships that she had was from her mother and father. For that to be where she learned how to approach relationships from was immensely profound. It was in her psychological makeup to want to be there for her suitor and to make things right. To go to the ends of the earth to prove herself so whomever she was with at that time would see that she was worth it. But the more she tried to prove herself, the more she devalued herself in the eyes of her suitor, much the same way as her mother had done.

This would place pressure on already exploitative men to leave as they felt like the relationship had gotten out of control. Drama would ensue but drama is what Sophia had been raised in; the constant back and forth so in a sense, it probably felt like home. She would get out of one relationship, weaker, and more hurt, attracting a savior to help her with her problems. He would come to the rescue and things would be good for a while…until a relapse, a reminder of a past relationship, an insecurity that either one of them faced (many times, the savior psychology of her male suitors was a way of compensating for their own internal insecurity or problems), and continue the perpetual cycle of defeat and discontent. In college, this only compounded for Sophia. Each relationship brought along a newfound happiness that was short lived because she could never let go of her previous relationship. She could never let go of criticizing the things she had done wrong and the areas where she had been unable to prove herself. Sophia was facing such a substantial threat to her well-being. She felt like she was nothing and meant nothing, and when a person feels like that, what do they have to live for?

The inadequacy of self is a disease. What it leads to is feelings of fear, pain, guilt, and hate; an overwhelming sense that life is worse than it actually is. Most people view life as something that affects them. The reality is that we affect life. We have the ability to craft our own experiences, in a broad sense to create the lives we desire. We are not less than worthy; we are individuals with a wealth of potential and talents that can exceed our wildest imaginations. Connecting with the understanding of how valuable we truly are has benefits that words do no proper justice in describing. When we escape what society or our upbringing has laid out for us as an extreme preoccupation on living completely in the moment, being totally consumed with what's next, or living deep in the past, we can rid ourselves of this inadequacy.

We have to consider each aspect of time equally; the past, the present, and the future. We tend to live our lives in one or two of these zones, but never all three. We can be consumed in right now, living each day as if it were the last. Or, we can be totally consumed in the past, blaming history for our trials and tribulations. We may not realize that those extremities have powerful effects on us right now and in the future. Each of these zones will help us to understand ourselves. Through proper focus on the past, present, and future, we can build our own adequacy. We are not dependent on where society, our parents, or other external factors say we should be. When we don't compare ourselves, we grow in our own independence. When we consider how each aspect of time has influenced and will influence our lives, without a disproportionate emphasis on one over the other, we stop disliking where we are and begin to create where we want to be. The *past* is what we should use to understand why we are the way we are. The *present* is what we should use to position ourselves for what is next. And the *future* is what we should use to keep us aware of what we intend to achieve.

The past is the most extensive database of information. The present and the future offer little to one seeking to understand themselves and their current position in life. When we look to the past, we are indeed informing our existence of whom we are and why we are. These are the experiences that we should use to break the cycles of our problems and forge our paths towards a happier life. Because previous segments have commented on the importance of the past, the following chapters will be centered in the present and the future.

3 | THE PRESENT: PT. I

"If you stay ready, you don't need to get ready."
- Will Smith

This view takes a page from the classic, *The Ant and the Grasshopper* fable. During the warm months of the year, the grasshopper spent his time singing and dancing in the grass. The ant, however, gathered food and leaves for the upcoming winter. When the winter arrived, the grasshopper starved and froze while the ant stayed warm and satisfied. This story reminds us that preparation is the best way to take advantage of opportunities; whether they exist now or will exist later. Using the moments we currently have to prepare for the future is the greatest way to ensure that we achieve our intended goals. Albert Einstein didn't learn everything he knew about quantum mechanics in one sitting. Mark Zuckerberg didn't create Facebook (formerly The Facebook) by himself nor in one coding session.

Rome wasn't built nor destroyed in a single day. These people and events that we hold in our minds as successes or indicative of some far off level of greatness were the unfolding of very iterative processes. They didn't just happen. To think that they did would be very short sighted. The views we hold of these people, places, and events required a significant amount of work. When we look at a person, we typically see just that, a person. We never see the story of that person. Instead of an extremely troubled woman with the hidden potential to influence millions and inspire generations, we see a blonde haired woman with bright red lipstick and a beautiful body named Marilyn Monroe. Instead of a palace built for the cherished love of a man's life that took sixteen years to build, we see the Taj Mahal. Instead of these processes, we see the outcomes, never fully acknowledging the fact that everything was created by interrelated actions. These backgrounds show the importance of investing the time we have into positioning ourselves for the future. Without them, the Taj Mahal would have never been created. Marilyn Monroe would never have inspired millions through her artistry. And Einstein's groundbreaking intellect would have never seen the light of day. The history of all things we hold near and dear is just that - a history...of building, of creating, and of positioning.

Every once in a while, we meet someone who leaves a spectacular impression on our lives. One such person that I recall is Justin. Justin was a student that I attended college with. I was first introduced to him when launching an investment partnership on campus. A friend thought that he would be a good addition and needless to say, he was right. Meeting Justin was like taking your first sip of alcohol. No one likes their first sip of alcohol. It's too strong, the taste is horrible, and people really can't justify why they're drinking except that everyone else is doing it and saying "keep going, keep going!" Justin's personality was very strong and he couldn't give two shits about what you thought of him. And like alcohol, my friend recommended him so I assumed he couldn't be too bad. My friend was right and pretty soon, Justin and I found ourselves talking and collaborating more. Interacting with Justin was thought provoking, stimulating, and just outright fun. And like so many of our first experiences with alcohol, I found myself wanting to interact more. I became less sensitive to the "two shits" attitude and began to really value the experience.

Justin had ideas that he could talk about for days, but beyond ideas, he had a means to implement them. Nothing seemed to get in his way for too long because his ingenuity would always trump the challenges he faced. He is one of those people who when you're around, you *know* anything is possible. An overwhelming sense of commitment, intelligence, and ambition radiates from who he is. Interacting with Justin will make you feel like he has the answer to any problem; even though he would be the first to tell you that he doesn't. I remember having meetings with Justin that I would leave from feeling particularly energized. I would go home and get so involved in work without knowing why and it was because I just felt good. I felt like a trillion bucks having left those meetings with him. One trillion dollars is beyond the million dollar dream; it surpasses what people believe they are capable of achieving. It is something that you imagine would come with a lot of burden but at the same time provide you with so much freedom. What do I do with it? Enrich the world, buy this or that, invest here or there? One trillion dollars will make you question who you are, what you're here for, how will you better the world, what will you do that is amazing? And that is what Justin does whether he knows it or not; he makes you stare those questions square in the face and he inspires in you, the confidence to answer them. He is Mr. Trillionaire.

Mr. Trillionaire

Justin was a part of the university's crew team. He had fairly modest beginnings. His high school was mixed, he got along with almost everyone, and was strong academically. JUstin grew up in a middle class family with both parents together. At the start of college; his life was eating, sleeping, and rowing. At least until his back injury which prevented him from ever rowing again. As bad as an injury sounds for any athlete, oddly enough, the inability to row provided Justin with the ability to pause and reflect on his life. He became more engaged on campus through extracurricular activities, bootstrapping an ailing club into the top finance organization on campus in a matter of months. He began to build products and businesses while consulting startups on how to grow.

Among his many creations, he constructed aquaponics systems and a portable solar charger for anything that uses a USB port. He consulted with businesses ranging from custom clothing startups to mobile applications for the energy regulation of homes to financial services firms. Justin's life was consistently breaking new barriers. Each time you talked to him, it seemed like he had completed one project and began another. Fathoming exactly how all of these things had come into play was a task in itself. But, like all of the greats, Justin used his present moments to position himself for the future.

After Justin injured his back, he took a deep dive into himself. It was definitely a new world for him; he now had the time to read, socialize, and explore. And he used that time very wisely. As a finance major, he decided to find clubs that interested him with their goals and actions. He couldn't, but what he did find was a club that had fallen out of favor. One that he could mold into something great. It just so happened that others were also looking for the type of club that Justin wanted to create and they wanted to be a part of its building process too. So they planned what it would look like and what value they would add. With a team of highly motivated students and an untapped need on campus (the product of a process in itself), the club took off and became the most successful finance organization at the university. But Justin didn't stop there. He parlayed the experience gained as president into a six-month co-op[1] at a Fortune 500 finance company, which became an incubator for him. What he did beyond his day-to-day job functions as an analyst was simple yet profound. He read.

He read countless articles, books, and publications on a variety of topics. He studied 3-D printing and read about meditation. He read about Steve Jobs, about startups, about finance. He read about religion and about the power of the mind. He read about aquaponics systems and agriculture. Justin read and read and read about damn near everything. Not only did he read but if he found that something sparked his interest, he explored it further questioning people in the field. He became increasingly inquisitive and it paid off. He never stopped reading after his co-ops and I guarantee you that he never will. That fundamental desire to soak up as much information as possible has had tremendous benefits on his life and it is because he took the time to develop himself. By doing all of this, Justin expanded his opportunity set. He created multiple paths to explore and platforms from which to jump. Justin's success and happiness is more accessible because he has prepared for it by positioning himself through deep self-analysis and exposure to new information.

The best way to experience dissatisfaction with life is to procrastinate. Pushing off what we intuitively know we should do now, until tomorrow. This is a habit that many of us face and it can be extremely difficult to break. It is important to realize that procrastination is indeed a form of

---

[1] Drexel Co-op is a six-month employment in practical, major-related positions consistent with student interests and abilities.

mental conditioning. When we constantly push off the things that we should do, we are training ourselves. We are saying to our brain, "look, this can get done later," and then later comes and we don't do it. We continue to find ways not to get some dreaded or even exciting task done. The more we do that, the more we will continue to do it and excuse it in our minds as the appropriate course of action. Imagine if Justin had chosen to procrastinate instead of reflect or read or learn more about the things that interested him. What things are you constantly doing that take up unnecessary space in your life?

This question caused me to think a lot about the people I consistently spent time with. Friends, acquaintances, business partners, and even family. We have to recognize that the time we spend with people who don't support our greater good conflicts with our own progress and even the progress of others. We may feel like the things we do are fun or exciting but we need to question them. We may also feel like certain things that we do are boring and stifling, and we should question those activities as well. What is important is to ensure that whatever we invest our time in doing is worth it, and that it positions us for achieving the life we want. It isn't easy to break a procrastination cycle when it starts. Trust me, I know from experience. It's like a domino set; delaying one activity and engaging in something else that is more exciting then another and another. The experiences all compound and you find yourself consistently wondering "how did I get here?"

What follows is a series of experiences in what I call my GPoP or my "greatest period of procrastination" to date. It was full of financial irresponsibility, relationship recklessness, and erratic behaviors, all culminating in a personal struggle to break free from wasting my life away. I don't hold any regrets from my experiences, they were great cultivation periods in my life and without having gone through them, I would not be equipped with the tools I have today. What I do acknowledge, however, is that there came a time where I had to question them to see if they were truly adding any substantive value to my life. The truth is that, if I were to continue, their value would become increasingly marginalized. It was time for a change and to start considering my life in a different context than what I had over the eight month period of procrastination.

It is appropriate to note here that my GPoP occurred slightly after my third breakup with my girlfriend. It became the time in which I decided to more fully experience alcohol and partying. This also highlights the time that I was encouraged to get an American Express Gold Card that I was qualified for, to begin building credit. I wasn't a fan of credit cards in general and I opted for the American Express Green Card which, like the Gold Card, came with no preset balance. *I'm also going to preface what follows with the fact that I didn't begin drinking alcohol until I was 22.*

London

The first domino in my GPoP was London. My mom was a flight attendant, which enabled me to fly within the United States for free and outside of the states for lower rates (just paying the taxes on the flights). My friend, Kam was studying abroad in London and we had been in talks about visiting him for our respective Spring Breaks. However, when I was scheduled to go on vacation for the Spring, Kam would already be back in the states. So instead of visiting over my vacation, I decided to visit him during his Spring Break. I would get out of class on Thursday, catch a flight that evening and arrive back in Philadelphia on Sunday to go to class the next day. The icing on the cake was that I had just received my American Express Green Card a few days earlier. I even told my dad that I would be traveling and would like some spending cash so he deposited $800 into my account.

I booked a hostel that was a two minute walk from Kam's dorm in South Kensington for seventy dollars and paid for my flight that cost $175. Thursday evening came around and I found myself on a flight to London more ecstatic than ever. On the Friday morning that I arrived, Kam and I explored the city. We went to breakfast at Borough Market, shopping in Camden Town, journeying on the Underground, and dining in Piccadilly Circus. As the evening emerged, we went back to Kam's dormitory in South Kensington and got ready to party for the night. We went out to a few nightclubs and had quite a few drinks. At one point, we ended up singing in the street with a Saxophonist and getting on the bus with a random stranger who guided us to a strip club. Talk about noble activities.

We ended up at the club, paid a few pounds to get in and proceeded downstairs. It seemed like an upscale club and as we walked, Kam noted the hazards of London strip clubs. In the states, you could toss denominations of dollars that goes all the way down to one-dollar. However, in London, the lowest cash denomination was five pounds, or seven dollars. Despite that, we sat down and began to talk and watch the show before our eyes. Two women dressed in scantily clad clothing approached our table and sat down with us. As Francesca whispered in my ear about buying a bottle of champagne to secure a private room, I melted.

Already drunk, I ordered the $265 bottle of Moet & Chandon. The women walked Kam and I over to a room that was really just a heightened platform blocked off by transparent curtains. We shared some of the alcohol with the waiter and all began sipping it down. Midway through the bottle and amid some engaging conversation, Francesca began whispering in my ear again detailing to me how for two-hundred pounds, Kam and I would receive lap dances.

Before I knew what was going on, I found myself running outside in the rain. Drunk, disoriented, and searching for an ATM because I didn't have enough cash on me. Within five minutes, I was back at the club with about $300 worth of Great British Pound in my hand. I gave half to Francesca and half to the woman Kam was with. Because of this newfound wealth, we upgraded rooms, this time to a larger platform with transparent curtains. At this point, it was beyond apparent that I was drunk. I was probably slurring my words and I considered everything in pounds to be equivalent in dollars. When I ran to that ATM, my thought was "oh, two hundred pounds is just like two hundred dollars." How wrong I was. And how drunk I was; I never actually received a lap dance from Francesca. I was so f***** up that I actually ended up giving her one. I effectively paid $150 dance on someone else. Afterwards, Kam and I left and took a bus back to South Kensington. I went into my room in the hostel and passed out. Fade to black.

I woke up disoriented and to the sound of a vacuum cleaner in the room. It astounded me because the woman cleaning had to have been in the room for a while because she was vacuuming the back half. I was in such a deep state of sleep that I didn't notice her until the vacuum's sound became so consistent that it was like an alarm clock ringing. I was still a little drunk, which I realized when I woke up, saw the woman, and ran out of the hostel to Kam's. I left most of my belongings at his dorm because I was afraid that someone in the hostel would steal them. I arrived at Kam's and we recounted the night briefly. To the point where we discussed how much money was spent, our response was simply, "we're in London!" Now that it was Saturday and there was no looking back on the previous night's experiences, we continued on our journeys. We walked through Regents Park, took pictures on Primrose Hill, went to Parliament and saw Big Ben. We event had high tea at the Royal Marriott with some of the most spectacular views of the Thames river. Afterwards, we experienced the London Eye, purchasing matching jackets at a gift shop and then proceeding to a twenty-minute 4-D experience of the London Eye. We took the Underground back to Kam's place and on the way purchased some groceries for making dinner. I went to the Hostel and changed which was followed by us going to Edgeware Rd. to eat. We laid low that night as the next morning, I had a flight to catch back to the states. When I arrived back, I recounted the entire experience extremely happy. There was only one sour point; I had spent $1,571.47…excluding international transaction fees.

London

Time of Experience: Sixty Hours

Money Spent: $1,571.47

Alcohol Consumed: Unknown but way too much

Greatest Mistake: I spent money that I did not have and set myself up for my first credit card bill being late. Thank goodness that my mother bailed me out so I wouldn't become a delinquent within one month of getting a new credit card.

That was step one of me procrastinating and not taking the time to consider how my decisions would play out in the future. This was step two…

When Doves Cry

The Kappa's

For the most part, we've all had our Frat party experiences. Those crazy one-offs that you know will come back to haunt you one day. Some friend years later from college says "remember that time?" Well these were mine.

Kappa Party I

I don't remember much of this night, which goes to show you how much alcohol I had consumed. Having recently come back from a trip home where I experienced a shot of Fireball Cinnamon Whisky, I thought it would be a good idea to buy a bottle. With a taste like the atomic fireballs purchased from those twenty-five cent machines and a bite like a rattlesnake, I downed seventy five percent of a 25 ounce, 66 proof bottle. Not to mention whatever other alcohol I had that evening including the *Jungle Juice* and related concoctions typically consumed at Frat parties.

I found myself dancing and having a grand ol' time. At one point, my friends iterated to me that a girl looked at me and commented "I don't think so, he's too nerdy." It must have been my glasses, however, upon hearing that I began to freestyle rap, apparently out of nowhere. After that, there seems to have been no question as to whether or not I was nerdy (not that being nerdy is a bad thing). My friends also told me that I attempted to strip during the party in a widely open area. Once my pants came down, two of them were there to help me pull them back up and stop. I have been told that I have a tendency to want to get naked and dance during parties when I am extremely drunk.

One part of the night that I do remember, however, is being outside of the party and throwing up over a stone wall. Hurling away in pain and desperate for someone to help me. However, no one was outside and I was alone trying to rid my system of whatever toxins I had let into it. When I finished vomiting, I was done with the evening. I made my way back into the party and my friend's had to take me home.

Kappa Party I

Time of Experience: Six Hours

Money Spent: $16.75

Alcohol Consumed: Again, unknown but way too much

Greatest Mistake: I let myself get beyond the point of reason and began the process for not caring about my body nor the fact that people around me would have to take care of me after a certain point.

Kappa Party II

Kappa Party II was the solidification of my consistent desire to run away from people when I became drunk past the point of reason. The experience was much like any of the other parties that I had been to with alcohol. Drink, dance, repeat. I was probably on my fourth iteration of drink, dance, repeat when I started fading. I became extremely tired and really just wanted to go home. In my daze of falling in and out of sleep while other people continued to dance, I noticed that I didn't see my close friends. I got up and walked towards the front of the house and saw them on the sidewalk as I looked from the porch. They told me that they would be right back and for me not to go anywhere.

I went back inside and drank a little more alcohol and then received the bright idea from the liquor gods to run away. To provide you with some context on where this house was, it wasn't in the best of neighborhoods. It was in West Philadelphia, which was the place where most of our university's robbery text alerts had come from. Without my friends there, I ran. I ran to another friend's house deeper into West Philadelphia. My judgment was obviously impaired. When I made it there, I called up and asked for them to buzz me in. Finally arriving upstairs, I began blurting out drunken comments and laid on their couch to go to sleep. Pretty soon, my friends who had taken a break from the party earlier were searching for me.

Since we were all mutual friends, they called the people whose apartment I was at and began to head over. Sadly enough, this wasn't the first time I had ended up like this For some reason, I became highly paranoid and thought that my friends were upset with me so I tried to hide in a closet so they couldn't find and reprimand me. My friends pulled me out of the closet, we had a good laugh, and they took me back to my apartment.

Kappa Party II

Time of Experience: Four Hours

Money Spent: $0

Alcohol Consumed: Yet again unknown, but way too much

Greatest Mistake: I endangered myself by running through one of the roughest neighborhoods in the city and became another obligation for my friends.

I must admit that there were more fraternity parties that I attended but I was too drunk to remember them all and my friend's recollections are more of the same: either I was running away, free styling, or we were moving the party from the house into the city where I would buy everyone nonstop rounds of shots and drinks on my Amex. The parties were step two of me procrastinating and not considering exactly how detrimental my actions were to my own existence. I was harming my health, diving deeper and deeper into a financial black hole, and even ruining relationships with people, particularly my girlfriend who had to take care of me on more occasions than one.

The Clubs

What I came to realize about my experience in clubs was that I had no control of my spending and very limited control of my inhibitions while under the influence. One drink was enough to have me loose and feeling generous enough to buy drinks for friends, DJs, and people whom I had never met before. The clubs of Philadelphia are where I lost sight of the more important things in life through my preoccupation with living in the moment.

Noche

Noche became the preeminent bar that my friends and I would frequent. For a period, we were there every weekend. The music was great, Mia our server was the best, and I was always able to get my mix of Grey Goose and cranberry juice. My friend Marco and I were partners in crime. If one of us was out, we both were. Our very first joint experience at Noche further solidified that relationship. We went to Noche with a few friends and the place was packed. We were able to secure a table when we entered, which we housed as our own. The server, Mia (whom we were meeting for the first time) came over and asked us what we would like to drink. I handed her my Amex, opened a tab, and ordered five shots of Soco Lime. After that, the drinks didn't stop. We would all float between dancing and our home table. Every time the shots were down, I found Mia or she found me and another round was ordered. Glasses of Grey Goose and cranberry juice flowed like a waterfall. Drinks for my friends: Jack Daniels, Vodka, and more shots of Soco Lime. I had no clue what was going on except that people were having fun. At the end of the night, the check came. $180. I asked Mia what she would like her tip to be. She hesitated and I told her I knew she wasn't supposed to answer but I asked again. She said $100. And there it was. My signature below a $280 bill with a little less than half of it amounting to a $100 tip.

When Doves Cry

Noche

Time of Experience: Three Hours

Money Spent: $277.80

Alcohol Consumed: Shots, shots, shots!

Greatest Mistake: While I am sure that there are people who spend substantially more than that in a club on any given night, the fact was that I was spending money I didn't have nor did I expect to have anytime soon. The harsh reality was that I didn't have a job.

Vango

I was never a fan of ghetto clubs and parties. They never really fit what I was looking for. However, I decided to venture outside of my comfort zone one evening. I joined my friends in going to a club in the city called Vango Skybar & Lounge. Two large bouncers stood outside the entrance of Vango checking id. When entering, people walk up a set of stairs surrounded by walls that have lamps made out of used alcohol bottles. At the top of the stairs, there is an open bar area and a dance floor. Towards the back sit tables up on platforms in private sections. There is another floor up another set of stairs that leads to an additional bar and a lounge on the rooftop.

It sounds like a very nice place, however, the crowd told a different story. I wasn't feeling the club too much with my friends…until the alcohol started to pour.[2] Once again, I handed the bartender my card and opened up a tab. No shots this time; just full specialty drinks for all of my friends. The music began pumping and we all began to have a good time. Dancing, drinking, repeating. The club was slated to close in thirty minutes so we decided to head out soon. I couldn't get the bartenders attention so I walked over to another side of the bar. Ironically there was a woman there and we sparked up a conversation. We had a mutual connection since we were both from the south. She told me that she was there with her friends and that they

---

[2] It is important to note here that this was the signal of a dependency on alcohol in order to have a good time, something that I had never needed before.

were also attending school in the city. The check arrived a few minutes later and I falsely relayed to her that I was so drunk and asked if she could sign it for me. It was an ego show; the check was $180 not including the $30 tip she allocated that I would find out about later when I checked my statement.

The tactic worked; she called over one of her friend's and I called over my partner in crime. I opened up a new tab and we all ordered more drinks. They called over a few more of their friends and we did the same. We were drunk and having a good time. It was always hard to tell if Marco was drunk but I knew he had to be when we all were talking and I asked him if I should get a bottle of champagne. He sipped his glass of Jack Daniels and shrugged. And there it was again; a $200 bottle of Moët and Chandon with fifteen minutes left to go before the club closed. In that second round, we all drank the champagne, had Long Island iced teas, Grey Goose and cranberry juice, and more all to the tune of $445.

After leaving Vango, we all found ourselves in the cars of the girls that we had just met. Of course, not until after I had returned from running away for the first time that night. The girls had two cars. I curled up in the fetal position back of one of the cars while everyone else figured out how what was next. Somehow I ended up switching cars and heading to West Philadelphia with one of the girls. One of my friends who was supposedly less drunk than everyone else drove the other girl's car. I will spare you the elongated details. We rode to West Philadelphia, I threw up, ran away again, was found by a friend, and blacked out. I woke up in my boxer briefs at the same friend's apartment from the Kappa frat parties. To top it off, I had an award ceremony that I had to be at in an hour.

Vango

Time of Experience: Seven Hours

Money Spent: $656.13

Alcohol Consumed: Exorbitant

Greatest Mistake: Everything; spending too much, drinking too much, riding with a drunk driver, etc. I repeat…everything.

There was a period for about a month, where I was spending at least $600 per weekend. Food, drinks, socializing, etc., etc. At the end of the day, I had nothing to show for it besides a really good lesson. I am not downplaying the fun I had and my learning, but it shouldn't have taken me $12,000 to learn not to spend money that I didn't have. That was an expensive lesson to understand not to drink, and not to consider my spending habits. By the end of that four month fiasco, I had spent $1,791.57 at Noche alone, not including other clubs, alcohol, dining experiences, and purchases. For more perspective, Noche costed me over two times my monthly rent.

In terms of preparation, I was setting myself up for failure. I was a junior in college with a $12,000 credit card bill and no means of paying it off. I had no job, my parents themselves weren't in the best financial position, and I had other bills to pay like tuition and utilities. I evaded American Express for as long as I could. Hiding my bill from my mom, making excuses, and talking to the company to push back the payments. Eventually, I received a notification in the mail that my account had been cancelled and that my failure to pay rendered a collection agency being assigned to obtain the back payment.

What I was doing by being so financially irresponsible was procrastinating. I was pushing back everything that I knew should have been doing; saving and investing for my future, building strong and genuine relationships with people, learning about my field of study, exploring my passions, and more. All of that was pushed back and it was sad. It was sad to see all of the potential to grow, to expand my consciousness, to develop myself, and cultivate a greater life wasted away by irresponsibility. It all left me with one of the greatest confusions and lacks of satisfaction with myself and my life that I had ever faced.

4 | THE PRESENT: PT. II

When we choose not to procrastinate, we experience the opposite effect of dissatisfaction. We condition ourselves to get the necessary things done without making excuses or distracting ourselves so they don't get accomplished. Taking the time to work on that homework assignment, prep meals for the week, save ten percent of our check, or wake up a little earlier all help us in the future. The tradeoffs are minimal compared to that of procrastination. The more we do the things we need to, the easier it is to achieve the life we desire. There is no way of escaping this reality.

When the Patriots won the Super Bowl in 2001, 2003, and 2004; it wasn't by mere chance. The previous seasons, the management, coaching staff and players spent time developing the team, practicing fundamentals, and perfecting their strategy. In the five year period between 2000 and 2005, the Patriots were in 50% of the championships, winning each one of them. I admit that while I am not a Pats fan (they beat my home team in 2004), I realize that they stuck to a fundamental concept. They positioned themselves very well so when each season arrived, they would be ready to rise to the challenge. The Patriots did not procrastinate. Instead, they forced themselves to get up every morning, practice every day, eat healthy every meal, and maintain a regiment that kept them focused better than any other team. This is true for all individuals.

The more that we position ourselves; learning, developing, practicing, putting in the work and not pushing it off, the more we will experience the rewards of success. If we don't, we run the risk of living very unfulfilling and unsatisfying lives.

Recognizing that the moments we have right now are extremely important means that we have to keep our actions in check. We have to understand that everything we do will affect us at some point in the future. This exists for every decision, from making sure to call mom to say happy birthday to signing fifty checks for your employees to staying consistent in meditating each day. Instead of the time that I spent partying and wasting money, there were many more activities that I could have been engaged in that would have added substantially more value to my life.

How many of us are caught in that cycle; feeling like life is getting redundant because we keep doing the same things over and over and over again? We might be lost in a job that is unfulfilling, knowing that it isn't what we want to do for the rest of our lives. Staying in that dead end job isn't preparing you for your future in the best way. Or potentially remaining in a relationship waiting for your partner to end it because you're either too afraid to hurt their feelings or stand up on your own. That relationship will continue to decline further and further the more you postpone ending it. Maybe you're pushing back exercising because you don't have the time. And the more you push it back, the further you go down the path of not ever deciding to exercise.

Action doesn't require huge steps. It requires small steps and reminders along the way. You don't have to quit your job, immediately break off your relationship, or step into some huge workout routine. It is more important to take small steps to forge ahead on the path of fighting procrastination. Start with exploring new job opportunities or finding out what your passion is. Start with talking to your partner about the progression or digression of the relationship. Start with eating a piece of fruit each day or doing ten sit ups. Just don't get satisfied by the introduction; push ahead, step by step and soon you will find yourself procrastinating less and positioning yourself for the future more. There is nothing to it but to do it, so let's get to it. The present is what we should use to position.

5 | THE FUTURE

Using the future as a tool to remember seems counterintuitive. However, the future is ultimately where we will or wish to be at some point in our lives. By keeping that vision or those goals prominent in our minds, it acts as a reminder. It guides us to break through short-term barriers, remain focused, and achieve our goals. The future, when viewed as a reminder offers tremendous value to people who want to create their own happiness and experience better lives. When our alarm clock rings in the morning, it is a reminder. It is saying to us "get up, get up, you have things to do today!" Whether that is to go to school, to work, to make money, be productive, pay bills, or whatever; that repetitive and often times annoying beeping noise is telling you to "get your ass up and at it!"

A lot of us prefer to stay asleep, at least for a few more minutes. So we roll over and hit the snooze button, delaying the things we need to do so we can do what we want to do: dream. That logic is very backwards and the time we spend asleep is the time we could have invested doing something else that was more valuable. Many of us spend so much of our time sleeping and hitting the snooze button on our lives. We forget or choose not to remember that we have things to do. We get distracted by the pleasure that *now* offers. A few more minutes of sleep feels so good. If only we would have gotten to bed on time the night before. We should remind ourselves of our future constantly; keeping where we want to be prominent so we can continue to take the steps we need in order to get there. For our daily lives, the alarm clock is that reminder, encouraging us to wake up and get focused.

The same is true if we were to take a picture of a beautiful and expensive home to show ourselves what type of life we want to live. That exact home may not be the home of our future but it is a reminder to say, "Maybe I *should* save ten percent of my check instead of using it to buy that new phone that I don't need." That photograph is symbolic of something deeper. It reveals to us a sense of purpose and can spur the motivation necessary to push through a hard time. It isn't just a picture of a house; it is something to stop us from falling too far when we go astray and at the same time, something to keep us inspired and focused when things are going well.

The future is what we should use to remember. To remember what still needs to be done. To remember that we are on the path to what we desire. To remember that no matter what we may be experiencing at that moment, we will achieve the goals we set out to achieve. The benefits of this process have been experienced by anyone who failed a class and had to take it again. They were required to look towards their past to understand why they failed. They took that learning and started doing things differently. They paid attention in class differently, studied differently, potentially even changed up their professors. By doing this, they positioned themselves for class participation, homework, quizzes, and tests better. When those moments came around to take a test, they were more prepared and experienced higher overall satisfaction. Throughout that entire process, they used the future to remind themselves that they needed to pass that class.

Otherwise, their GPA would decline, they wouldn't be able to graduate, or their parents would reprimand them. A variety of different reasons informed them of the benefits or consequences of their ability to pass the class. Want to go out and party before not studying? Go to dinner with friends or enjoy a new movie? Want to get mentally prepared for studying before hitting the books? Then they would run the risk of not passing an assignment and ultimately the class. The future served as a reminder.

Conclusion

When we consider the three aspects of time, we have to be cognizant of the fact that we only have this moment to act. This is the moment that life will continue to be built on. Our lives will forever reflect the steps we took, and the one's we didn't. Remember that all we have is now, but integrated in now is the ability to understand what has been and the ability to create what will be. When we equip ourselves with this understanding, no longer are we exposed to the inadequacy of self. We will begin to act from confidence in our own abilities, depending on our own histories, and creating our own futures.

We expand our perspective to include and further develop the excellence of our existence. Without consideration of each of these aspects of time in balance, we may very well fall prey to society and subconsciously view our lives as insignificant or inadequate. That is not the case; in fact it is far from it. Why does all of this matter? Because you should know that you are valuable. You should know that you have talents that people will find benefits in whether you currently see what they are or not. It is important not to discount and discredit yourself because that only slows progress towards increased levels of happiness. Instead of maintaining the perspective of an inadequacy of self, we should strive to have a more developed sense of self.

Many times, what slows us from acknowledging how truly awesome we are is fear. We fear that we aren't perfect and that we will never be. That thought prevents us from progressing and taking the steps necessary to grow. We hear the notion "nobody is perfect;" something that I strongly, strongly disagree with. Perfection is dynamic and not static and that means *everything* is perfect. We live life in an ever unfolding perfection. If we claim something as imperfect, we are claiming that it can be better. Perfect *is* the state of being better and there is nothing that doesn't have the potential to be better. It is not the best but simply, better which is always available. If we are uncomfortable accepting that what is will not always be, then we are taking a very narrow view of life.

Everything is perfect, as everything is becoming. We never stop becoming and we never stop being perfect. The qualifier here is that existing in perfection means existing in becoming. You cannot stop becoming but you can slow it down or speed it up. By feeding into the notion that we are inadequate, we slow it down. By viewing ourselves as capable, considering the aspects of time in a balanced manner, and understanding how awesome we really are, we advance ourselves and can live in a state of perpetual perfection. We become unbound by what society has deemed adequate.

Escaping that view requires confidence. It requires the boldness to say "I have to live my life" and even the courage to say "I will start to take the steps necessary to become happier." Taking those risks of stepping into your own sense of self can seem like a huge risk, however, the biggest risk we can take is not to take one at all. We have more to lose by being complacent than we do by putting ourselves out there.

There are two main things that can breed complacency; the comfort that you're doing well or the fear of never being able to achieve something greater. For the former, it's important to get really comfortable with being uncomfortable. Challenging yourself to be more pushes you to do more. If you feel that you are doing well, question how you can do better. Be grateful for where you are but give yourself the respect of increasing your potential for your sake and for the sake of those around you.

For the latter, we cannot fear not stacking up. We must realize that there is not and never will be a point to stop. Your impact will outlive you and it is important to make it a significant one. The fear of never being able to achieve something, or achieve it to the level that someone else does is extremely comparative and it creates excuses that support stagnation. Be your own benchmark and refuse to let your perception of external or internal expectations hold you back from being what your potential can lead you to. You are not inadequate and it is about time that we were appropriately informed of the greatness of our own existence.

6 | HAKUNA MATATA

Introduction

Problems don't have to be barriers in our lives; they can be opportunities. We shouldn't have to worry about them consistently because they can and should be easily fixed. Why? Because people are awesome and we're worth it. We don't give ourselves enough credit. We spend more time worrying about the problems we have instead of the talents we have. The more time we spend acknowledging the issues, the problems, and the ways that life is a challenge, the more time we spend being an issue, a problem, and a challenge to ourselves. It ends up giving our problems more power. It is important to look at the problems we face and with certainty say that we will break their cycle. It is important to say, "Hakuna Matata."

Timon: Look, kid. Bad things happen, and you can't do anything about it, right?
Simba: Right.
Timon: Wrong! When the world turns its back on you, you turn your back on the world.
Simba: Well, that's not what I was taught.
Timon: Then maybe you need a new lesson. Repeat after me.
 {Clears throat} Hakuna Matata.
Simba: What?
Pumbaa: Ha-ku-na Ma-ta-ta. It means "No worries."
Timon: Hakuna Matata! What a wonderful phrase.

Pumbaa: Hakuna Matata! Ain't no passing craze.
Timon: It means no worries. For the rest of your days
Timon and Pumbaa:
>   It's our problem-free
>   Philosophy
Timon: Hakuna Matata!
Simba: Hakuna Matata?
Pumbaa: Yeah, it's our motto.
Simba: What's a motto?
Timon: Nothing! What's a motto with you? Ahh ha ha ha...
Pumbaa: You know, kid-- These two words will solve all your problems.

Hakuna Matata means no worries. It's a phrase which was taught to more generations than one through the movie the Lion King. Beyond just a line from a movie, it speaks to an acknowledgment of truth. Hakuna Matata is the recognition that "yes, something is challenging me right now but I won't let it negatively affect my life." That "I will, through my own resolve create a living experience that is happier and that breaks through whatever problems I may be facing because I can and because I deserve it."

Hakuna Matata is profound and it can have a dynamic impact on our lives. What types of problems are you going through right now that you should say Hakuna Matata to? What isn't worth your stress, what isn't worth your worry? What is, however, worth your peace of mind and happiness? When we're facing any problem, whatever it may be, sometimes we all need to just say "Hakuna Matata;" it means no worries, about anything ever- life will go on. Spending an exorbitant amount of time on our problems can be unhealthy. We become so ingrained in what our struggles are, we miss out on life. Counting the finite things that are wrong and missing the infinite things that are right. Let's all stop worrying and start living!

David V. Hunt

Excuses, Excuses

How many excuses are we going to make? For not reaching the level of life we want to? For not creating a solution because a challenge is too great? The most striking thing about excuses is that when we create them, it's extremely difficult to tell. However, when someone else makes an excuse for why they can't do something, we can call it out from a mile away. It is hard to see that we've made an excuse because we've become so good at it that it feels like there are these external barriers which prevent us from solving our problems. Often times, we build reasons into our lives for why certain things never work out no matter how hard we think we are trying.

These reasons eventually prevent us from removing the blockages from experiencing happier lives. Creating excuses blinds us to the deeper reality that we are in control. That we have more power than we think when it comes to creating solutions to the problems we face. We have to be honest with ourselves about what is real and what we have created. Our struggles, our problems, our successes, our happiness. All of these experiences are not void of our actions; we play a significant role in the emotions we experience. Being honest in understanding that role is extremely important, otherwise, we run the risk of continuing to live dissatisfied, unfulfilled, and disappointed, whether with our entire life or specific portions.

When I worked over the summer for a co-op during college, I developed a very unique relationship with one of the employees there. She had been working there for two years, immediately following her college graduation. To put it succinctly, she hated her job. She despised the people, thought they were incompetent, and detested the work. She believed that organization and communication within the firm was extremely inefficient and antiquated. When the person who originally hired her, someone who had become a great friend and mentor to her, left the firm it only made matters worse. Her mentor was replaced and very quickly fell into the same bucket as the rest of the people in the company. Being passed up for a promotion at the departure of her boss increased her frustrations and ultimate discontent with the company.

Others in the company were very clearly aware of her unhappiness although she did not think she wore her emotions on her sleeve. Her direct relationships with people became more rigid as she sought to maintain an air of extreme professionalism. What she didn't realize was that instead of being professional, her demeanor was viewed as extremely distant, cold, and at times rude. Employees of the firm could see it every day, on her face through her lack of smiles and the walls she put up while at work. What was particularly interesting about her perspective was that she was the only one who held it at such an extreme. There were many other people within the firm with their own disapprovals of others, however, they found ways to get along with each other, work well, and have productive synergies.

Beyond age, gender, race, and other demographic characterizations, I found one key difference between the way she approached work versus the way others in the office had approached it. She viewed work as a place to come, get things done, get paid, and leave. Many other viewed work as a place to come, chat a little, get work done, get paid, and leave. While I am sure there were more intricacies relative to specific individuals, the fact that other people gave attention to a little chatting was an attribute whose significance cannot be overstated. Over the prior two years of her employment, she became numb to her job. She became numb because there was nothing more filling her day than a responsibility, an obligation. She didn't have a sense of purpose or fulfillment beyond what her job description stated. So much so that it showed in her actions and emotions and even her facial expressions and mannerisms. There was nothing at work that she viewed as even remotely pleasurable. That had to be a very tough place to be in; spending eight hours a day, five days a week, each week with no stimulation and feeling unfulfilled. Almost twenty-five percent of her week, every week was nothing more than an obligation.

On the other hand, however, there were many people who enjoyed work. They may not have loved it, but they were very far away from the level of hate that she had for it. The difference was indeed the social aspect. Most people would chat a little. It was enough to forge friendships, create bonds, and make work feel a little less like a responsibility. They understood their environment and created ways to adapt to and within it, crafting their own enjoyment. They chose not to go the route of extreme dissatisfaction with their job. They didn't make the excuse that they didn't like the people, didn't like the work, or anything else, and stick with it. Everyone faces times where they run into people or activities that they don't like to interact with. In this case, however, the other employees didn't spend time focusing on how bad those relationships were. They didn't waste time considering everyone and their faults nor did they spend too much time criticizing how they didn't like the work they were doing.

They adapted and created things that they did like so they could approach those situations better. But no one just knows how to adapt; how to learn and adjust. She spent two years believing that her professionalism would outweigh the need to be social. It didn't. Work environments are not zero sum games. They require a degree of balance to operate within them. Constant disappointments with not feeling like her work and logic created the results she wanted built an emotional retaliation to the firm. Embedded in her persona, her demeanor, and even the tone of her voice was disgust, and everyone noticed it, except for her. She thought that she was being direct when she actually was perceived as being annoyed. And when project dates would get missed by her superiors or people would fail to respond to emails, the anger grew. She became a robot; expecting the same shit every day and responding to it the same shit way.

When I initially came in as a co-op, I was afraid to approach her. From my very first day, and without any background commentary about her from any other co-worker, she always seemed upset. She would let out a long sigh each time she came in and sat down in the morning as she popped an Advil. She was always very distant and it was apparent that she did not like her job. As time progressed, we slowly began to develop a relationship and share more information with each other. I came to realize her true feelings towards the firm and the reasons for those feelings. It was the constant missed emails, late meetings, jobs not being done, personality flaws, the list went on and on...and on. We had many conversations and "stress-relief" sessions after work.

Ninety percent of our conversations were in relation to something negative about work and ninety-three percent of the commentary was her talking. It was heartbreaking to see someone so young with so much distaste in their life for a job already. She had just come out of college two years prior and was already more cynical than any other person I had ever met. The cynicism and sarcasm extended into her personality, to where I found myself being criticized for trying to bring humor to situations. And I wondered, how many other people are out there feeling that? Caught up in jobs that they don't like and building this repository of hatred towards people, responsibilities, society, and life. I'm sure she wasn't, isn't, and won't be the only one. I remember thinking that her experience over the past two years was so negatively skewed that it would be carried into her future employment and life experiences. One of the conversations that we had brought a lot of issues to the forefront.

She was highly stressed and relaying what had occurred throughout the day. Before she could finish, she interrupted herself, let out a sigh, and said "I hate this place." I asked why she couldn't adapt to it, to the people, and find something valuable. Her response: "I just can't, it's not me." So I pressed on asking what she meant and she said that she really just couldn't stand her job or the people and that it was no use anymore. Her experience had numbed her to reality, so much so that she was making excuses as to why not to try. Making excuses for why she couldn't try and view the people differently. I don't mean to say that the job was correct for her in any substantial way, however, her emotions were so wrapped up in pessimism that any optimism with work, life, or a different job had waned.

She had spent two years with a negative view of the people and not in any one of those nearly ninety weeks of work including holiday, vacation, and sick time had she truly attempted to change her view of the people or the work. Not in any one of those weeks had she said "okay, maybe I am making this bigger than it actually is." Instead, she decided to do what was comfortable and say "these people don't know what they are doing" and "this work sucks" so I will just deal with it. It wasn't that she couldn't change the way she approached the situation, it was that she wouldn't and that she didn't want to. She had grown into her way of doing things, of existing as someone whose job it was to just show up. It became so clear when we talked about ways to potentially change the situation that she didn't want to grow. There wasn't even avoidance in those conversations, it was just backlash that attempting to have a better experience at work wasn't worth the effort. Her comments repeatedly became "Well, as long as I don't get fired I suppose I'm alright."

If not for the sake of her mind, for the sake of her health to attempt something to reduce that stress! When are we going to stop making excuses for our own progress? When are we going to have our hunger for greatness outweigh our satisfaction with mediocrity? We cannot approach life like it is something that happens to us. A big piece of our locus of control is internal; we are the ones that affect life. The things that we experience are in some way, shape, or form related to the choices that we make. That responsibility scares us; it is too much power or authority. If we were to consider the consequence of every action; making a left instead of a right, reading a book instead of watching a television show, partying instead of going to a lounge, texting instead of talking, etc., we would go stir crazy.

But that doesn't detract from the basic reality that our actions have consequences. Our life is in our hands and when we realize that we are the ones with the power to create happiness in our own lives, we come to an understanding that we have no excuses. There is no reason why we shouldn't be happy. There is no reason that we shouldn't solve our problems. And that is not something that a lot of us are comfortable with. Excuses feel so good. They protect us, and they give us a way to say "it wasn't my fault," "God didn't want it to happen," it wasn't meant to be," and on and on…and on.

We have to be brutally honest with ourselves in understanding the reasons that we decide our problems are too great to be dealt with appropriately. If not, we will continue to blame what is "out there" for our challenges. Our parents, our childhood, or our situation. But no, those are the experiences that we should use to inform our existence, not the ones to perpetually create it. Our past is a great tool that can be used to create the life we want. We spend so much of our time wasted, dreaming for better and wanting it with all of our might. As James Froude iterates, "you cannot dream yourself into a character, you must hammer and forge yourself into one."
We must want better more than our biases and fears. We must want greater more than what the strength of our convictions and presuppositions say it takes to achieve that greatness. We must stop making excuses. And that begins with taking a deep look at our life, seeing the excuses that we have

put up to slow us down from tackling them, and simply saying "Hakuna Matata, let's get busy."

7 | THE GRATITUDE PARADOX

When I was younger, my mother would always buy me clothing sets that matched in color. To be honest; I couldn't stand them. I didn't want to be the kid at school with blue shorts, a blue shirt, and blue shoes. I wanted a little contrast, you know funk it up a little. As I grew older, she began to notice this and started adding variation to the clothes that she purchased. Most of the time, I did like the clothes, however, I always saw a different variation that I liked better. I was grateful for what she had purchased and for the effort that she had put into buying me clothes. At the same time, I wasn't satisfied. I knew that there was something edgier and more appropriate for my own fashion profile. She always took this as a sign of being ungrateful; however, I knew that wasn't the case. I was experiencing a paradoxical relationship; one that has been responsible for countless achievements throughout history.

If we look at great inventors, business magnates, oratory leaders, etc., they were never satisfied. However, they retained significant appreciation for the tools, knowledge, and environment they did have in order to create greater things. The Gratitude Paradox is a relationship between being grateful for a particular situation, circumstance, or outcome while never being satisfied by that same experience. This paradox has supported ambition, innovation, achievement, and progress for generations. It is one of the most valuable relationships that we can come to understand and integrate into our lives. While many people are indeed happy, that does not detract from the fact that there are greater levels of happiness to experience.

Alternatively, there are also many people who feel challenged by their lives, or in some cases indifferent towards it. This paradox acknowledges that it is important for us to consider the things we have to be grateful for while looking ahead to the things that we eventually want to come to appreciate. When we approach life with this paradox in mind, at least partially embedded in it, we create an opportunity to experience greater. A greater degree of happiness, of joy, of impact; ultimately a greater degree of life. We may already be happy but that doesn't mean we can't be happier.

A few questions may come to mind. Why is it important that we should try to be happy and then attempt to be happier? What if we are already happy? Happiness is a very natural state that we diminish contact with as we grow older. The things most resembling our natural state in life are those that are the most valuable. Think to some of the things you love now; how much of it is rooted in your childhood-to-adolescent moments of excitement. Traveling, eating certain foods, building and playing with Lego's®, reading, etc., etc. Those fostered a very natural sense of happiness and satisfaction with life.

Remember that annual trip to the Poconos where you and your family would all play instruments, tell stories, dance, laugh, and just have a good time? You felt something very real and very special about that time; you didn't force that feeling, it was just there. It was happiness. These experiences provide us with a sense of joy and purpose, they make us feel good, and have positive impacts for the people around us. These are just a few of the reasons why we should try to be happy and if being happier expands our sense of purpose, our feeling good, and the positive impacts we have on the people around us then it is something we should invest our time in. If we question why we should be happy, perhaps it is because we have grown used to feeling unhappy. Feeling like life is full of defeat or challenges or problems is simply contrary to the truth. Happiness is and will forever be an emotional experience that yields increasing benefits for our lives.

Happiness is a function of exposure, much like any emotion we feel. Through our different experiences, we perceive varying degrees of happiness that are based on the impacts our past has had on our lives. In the sixties, when my dad was growing up in Philadelphia, he and his siblings didn't know what 'being poor' was. Everyone in the neighborhood had the same things, ate the same foods, and engaged in the same activities more or less. They were all relatively content and at comparable levels in life. Their frame of reference was that they were just living life. They weren't poor, they weren't rich, they were just living. And that limited exposure was the foundation for how they would carry themselves throughout the remainder of their lives.

In the context of what would have been a broader view of their socioeconomic status, my father's family was struggling. Many times, they were unable to eat, were caught in gang territories, and deprived of some the most basic rights that we now all take for granted. It wasn't until they were exposed to something outside of their own modern lives were they able to think beyond their situation. As my dad grew up, he took a job driving around a Mr. Softee ice cream truck. It was his responsibility, each evening, to drive through the neighborhoods that he was used to experiencing, the poor side of Philadelphia. Afterwards, he would drop the truck back off at the local Mr. Softee warehouse. The route was the same his first few weeks until staffing ran low, which expanded the areas that he had to service.

He was assigned an additional route; one that he would run during the day while the sun was up. During the evening, he was still charged with driving through the rougher neighborhoods. During the day, however, he drove through areas that he had never been in before. There were large houses, children playing outside, and adults relaxing on porches. There were mansions, smoothly paved roads, and lawns with fresh cut grass. There weren't any broken down cars on the side of the street, no gangs, no drug houses, and no trash on the sidewalks. It was a completely different world. As he went along his route, he realized that he had spent most of his life in a silo. Up until that point, he didn't know that houses that large had even existed. He didn't know that people didn't work in their jobs all day, and he didn't know that he was poor. He did now.

My dad realized that everything that had been his life up until that point was so limited. School hadn't taught him anything about socioeconomics or upward mobility. His parents were as troubled as he was because they had no access to the pleasantries of "the other side" either. Life hadn't taught him anything about what he had seen. Beyond what he saw that day, what more was there to see? The first evening after visiting the affluent neighborhoods, as he drove through the poorer ones he made a promise to himself. He promised that one day, he would be able to work whenever he wanted, that he would have a nice house, and that he wouldn't be limited by what he didn't have access to.

It is so easy for us not to know. To not know how sad we may actually be. To not know how happy we can be. To not know what opportunities we can create. Who knows if the happiness my dad experiences now, after having started his own business and achieving a notable level of success is simply another silo. How much happier can he be? For reasons of fear, comfort, ignorance, or not having been exposed to different experiences, cultures, and thought processes. As we embark on our life journeys, we have to remember to never be satisfied while at the same time remaining grateful for what was, is, and will be.

There are things that we don't know, happiness we've never experienced, and joys that we have never imagined. We don't have to settle for what we know now and the happiness we currently have. We can always challenge ourselves to experience greater lives regardless of how good or bad they may be at the current moment. We have to explore the things about ourselves and our lives that we don't know by exposing ourselves to different experiences. The effect is happiness. What my dad has done since then has been to remain grateful for all of his accomplishments while never being satisfied and continue engaging with growing, developing, and breaking the barriers of his challenges. That moment as an ice cream truck driver was something that propelled him to grow beyond his circumstances. It was something that showed him that what he lived in was a problem and that he could excel beyond it. It provided him with one of the most profound Hakuna Matata moments of his life.

The Gratitude Paradox requires two basic steps; (1) to be grateful for a situation, circumstance, or outcome and (2) to never be satisfied with that experience.

Gratitude

Be grateful for everything. Every situation, every experience, every "negative" thing that occurs in your life has value. It is up to your perception to frame your life in the appropriate context from which to be grateful. Without acknowledging the value that each of our experiences has, we fail to find a deeper meaning to them. A meaning that ultimately will create a path for us to progress through the challenges we face. The importance of gratitude cannot be overstated. It is something that enlivens us and enables our minds to approach situations from a position of power. We refuse to be negatively critical of whatever it is that is going on and instead find a way to leverage our perception against our situation. Problems come and go, but we will always have our mind to depend on. If we can condition ourselves to be grateful in the face of any challenge, we expedite the process of creating solutions and ultimately more happiness in our lives. It positions you to solve them more effectively and efficiently; with less stress and more perceptiveness about their magnitude.

Less Stress

How many times have we experienced some problem that we constantly think about how bad it is? We all have a tendency to do that. Our car broke down, our child was in an accident, our parents are getting divorced, our job is downsizing and the list goes on. I am not saying that these aren't problems; but the more time we spend noting how bad they are, the more time we spend stressing ourselves out. Our view on these problems is one-sided to the negative and that is what is truly bad. One-sided optimism is equally detrimental because we become disillusioned to the fact that we are actually facing a challenge. Instead, we should see how these problems can be valuable for us without losing sight of the fact that they actually need to be handled. The way to begin this process is by being grateful and the effects that gratitude has on lowering our stress is significant.

More Perceptiveness

We blow our problems out of proportion. One problem encourages us to consider what else in our lives is going wrong and then we bucket everything together as if it were all the same. Gratitude acknowledges the value that we can derive from a particular situation. It maintains clear links to specific challenges and prevents us from trying to group everything together into one huge mess. Gratitude informs us of specific problems and enables us to say "okay, this isn't that bad. Let me not blow my top off about it." By doing that, we gain clearer insight into the magnitude or significance of the problems that we face.

Ultimately, gratitude changes your perspective on the problems you experience. Instead of just asking "why did this happen to me;" you deepen your understanding by also asking "what can I learn from this" and "what value can it have in my life?" Gratitude gives you power: it creates the base from which you can approach your problems more effectively. The act itself may not solve your problems but it will definitely put you in a state of mind that makes solving them easier. Why? Because instead of spending all of your energy acknowledging the fact that there is a problem, you invest your energy acknowledging the understanding that you can gain from the issue. Said Albert Einstein "Problems cannot be solved at the same level of awareness that created them." If we are stressed about a situation, we can't fix it appropriately in that stressed state of mind. We are irrational, impulsive, and ill-informed of how challenging that situation really is. We have to redefine our perspective if we are to correct our problems and the most fundamental step in that process is to be grateful.

In 2004 after graduating from middle school, I vacationed with my step-mom and father in Toronto, Canada. In a sense, it was a rite of passage journey; I was heading to high school soon. I felt like I was ready to explore the world and meet new people. It was an exciting time for me and we were able to experience a lot in Canada. We went to markets, festivals, rode on tour buses and boats, and immersed ourselves in the culture. While there, tiny black bumps began to sprout up on my tongue. They didn't hurt but they felt awkward. We all thought that it was because I was eating too much sugar so I drank a lot of water to get rid of them. I also felt low on energy throughout the day but at night, my energy would randomly spike up. We didn't make too much of it until I traveled back home and saw my mom. She looked at my tongue, smelled my breath, and immediately knew something was wrong. Within a few moments of seeing her, we were on our way to the hospital to check it out further.

When we arrived, the doctor probed me with questions, smelled my breath, and drew blood to run tests. I was checked into the hospital that same day so the staff could keep an eye on me. As we walked towards the room that I was assigned to, I was so confused. I had no idea what was going on, why I had to be checked into the hospital, nor when I would be released. I couldn't stand the fact that I had to have my blood drawn because I was so afraid of needles. Despite my misunderstanding of what was occurring, I was directed to my room while my parents talked with the nurses at the front desk. I went into the restroom to urinate but for some strange reason, I couldn't. Liquid was flowing out from my body and from the right area, but it wasn't urine. It was blood. I panicked. I pulled the nurse call string and told her what was going on. She rushed in, I was connected to an IV, more blood was drawn, and fluids were pumped into my body. In a matter of moments, what I knew as my life completely stopped. Everything I thought about living a long life, everything I thought about going to high school, everything I thought about being healthy, being a kid, and just living came to a screeching halt. And there I was. Fourteen years old, feeling alone and lost and like my life had just changed forever. And it had.

Within a few days, I was diagnosed Aplastic Anemia, a rare blood disorder. The reason my breath smelled so terrible was because I was bleeding internally and I had dried up blood sitting stagnant in my body. The tiny bumps on my tongue were actually all over my body. They were tiny bruises forming because my platelets weren't producing in large enough quantities to protect me from my daily activities. The average person has around 200,000 platelets in their body preventing excessive bleeding. When I was checked in, I had two-thousand and was on the cusp of a coma. My red and white blood cell levels were extremely low in production and my immune system was failing. In essence, my bone marrow was experiencing a deficiency where it wasn't producing enough blood and platelets to keep me healthy. I ended up going through a brief bout of chemo therapy and almost had to receive a bone marrow transplant from my brother. I remember the point where I cried when the doctor was discussing the prospects of having a transplant. He said two words that made me walk out of the room and the tears started to fall. "Death rate." I never actually heard what the survival rate for the operation was though. All I knew was that there was a chance that I might die during it. And that was enough for me to break down.

Despite that fact, I continued with the tests, infusions, and medication. Throughout the entire experience, I received a tremendous amount of support. My family visited multiple times, people prayed, doctors and nurses ran tests, and I went through therapies. I was hopped up on Benadryl, sometimes morphine, magnesium oxide, cyclosporine, and hydrocodone. After being in the hospital for ten days, I was finally released. However, I had to have a catheter installed in my chest and was sent home with a portable IV to keep pumping fluids through my system. Nurses would visit the house weekly to draw blood and run tests. I had to be homeschooled for two years, missing my freshman and sophomore year of high school for fear of getting bruised or becoming sick, and having to be hospitalized again. On multiple occasions, I would wake up with chills or a bruise and have to be taken back to the hospital to get a blood or platelet transfusion. Throughout the entire experience; I faced a wide variety of emotions ranging from being shocked to confused to fearful but I could only bring myself to say one thing about the entire experience. And it was something that I continue to say today, which is thank you.

Thank you to the nurses who drew my blood even though I was afraid. Thank you to my family and my friends for being there every day. Thank you to the doctors who diagnosed me and were patient and understanding during such an involved time. Thank you to the chemotherapy for trying to help me through, and correct whatever imbalances were occurring in my body. Thank you to every single medicine that I was on regardless of the taste or the symptoms; for being there for me when I was shivering, when I was overheated, when I was in pain...when I was in need. Thank you to the service dog who would sit on my bed and lick my hands letting me know that everything would be alright. Thank you to my mom who took so many days off from work and to her co-workers who donated their sick time.

Thank you to my father for his artwork that energized the room and my spirit. To the Fresh Prince of Bel-Air who kept me laughing and to Aplastic Anemia for showing me how valuable life is. "Thank you;" it's something in our lives that we should never be able to say enough of.

Even though I faced so many emotions of fear and confusion throughout my experience, my ability to remain grateful remained consistent. Each time a nurse would draw my blood, I would respond in kind. Each time the doctor would leave from talking us through what was occurring, I would say thank you. That gratitude helped me get through one of the toughest times in my life because it redefined my perspective on the challenges that I was facing.

Had I considered how bad my situation was each day, I would have never had any positive energy to wake up and smile. I would have given up hope and set myself up for a very horrible ten days in the hospital. Instead, I took the time to appreciate every aspect of what was occurring; my fear, my confusion, my laughter, my family, everything. Without that, I don't know where I would be today. Those acknowledgements were extremely influential in my life because they conditioned me to have a resilient outlook. They taught me that no matter how difficult or improbable things become, "you better approach it the best way you can." There was no use in complaining, no use in being negative, no use in giving up.

All that would have done was stifled me. But what gratitude did was encourage me. It made me more aware of what I had within my control. And that awareness caused me to say "alright, I can't control certain aspects of this situation. So I will let the doctors, nurses, and medicine do what they need to do. And I have to do what I can." What I could do was read Robert Kiyosaki's *Rich Dad Poor Dad* and learn about investing. What I could do was watch the Fresh Prince and laugh and enliven my spirit. What I could do was consider whose lives my story could impact. What I could do was plan to donate toys and books to the children in the hospital when I got out to make their experiences a little easier.

I could do so many things other than worry and among them was being grateful for the value that I could derive from my situation. Gratitude enabled me and it has a similar effect for all of us. When we are grateful about whatever challenges we face, we make it a hell of a lot easier to approach them. We must all be grateful.

Never Be Satisfied

Not being satisfied fuels the desire for achieving greater life experiences. It doesn't care about what problems you are currently facing; it simply says "I'm ready for next great thing." We should never be satisfied. Without satisfaction, we don't quit. We keep going, moving, breaking through the barriers we knew we had and the ones we thought we didn't. Without satisfaction, we grow in our awareness that we can truly achieve anything we desire. This lack of satisfaction is extremely important in the Gratitude Paradox. It is the motivation for solving our problems and forging ahead. It is an inexhaustible reservoir that respects no challenge and backs down to nothing. Never being satisfied is that voice that all of us need, to push us to keep going and create the happiness in our lives that we desire.

Alternatively, when we are satisfied, we prevent ourselves from seeing key opportunities. The chance to progress, innovate, grow, solve challenges, etc. When we become satisfied, we become lethargic. It is as if we ate so much food that our stomach expanded beyond the point of additional intake. All we can do afterwards is manage our way to the couch, turn on the television, and fall asleep. Many of us do that every day. We fail to finish a project because we're comfortable with where we are. We muddle through our job because we're okay with it being mediocre. Or we stop being spontaneous in our relationship because we've grown accustomed to the norm. Satisfaction can have devastating effects on our lives because it invites us to a world of extreme comfort. We have to refuse to be satisfied so we can be motivated to solve our problems and grow in experiencing greater levels of happiness.

Motivation for Solving Problems

If we refuse to be comfortable with our problems, we will begin to create solutions for them. We will recognize the need for a change and develop ways to institute that change. Whenever we're uncomfortable with anything; a sitting position, a grade on a test, the temperature in a room, etc., we do something about it. Whether that something is to reposition, study, or change the thermostat, at the very least, we initiated an action to solve those problems. Not being satisfied gives us the motivation to approach our problems because we view them as malleable. Being alright with the consistent challenges that we face may mean that we perceive them as fixed and as a permanent part of our lives. There is no problem that cannot be solved but there are many solutions that are not created because of our own acceptance of them as insurmountable.

Motivation for Greater Happiness

Dissatisfaction is fuel. It refuses nonchalant acceptance of whatever *is* and provides a foundation to create what will be, even if current circumstances are favorable. Indeed, a lot of people are happy with their lives. I know that I am. I have a fantastic family, phenomenal friends, I love my self-awareness, and my past experiences. I genuinely love my life and am extremely thankful for what has happened, is happening, and will happen later. However, I realize that there are greater levels of happiness to connect with. I have heightened levels of value to add to people's lives, different things to learn and be exposed to, and other people to encourage and believe in. That lack of satisfaction fuels and encourages me to focus on creating increasingly positive impacts in people's lives.

Yin Yang

The combination of gratitude with not being satisfied, enables us to experience the true benefits of the Gratitude Paradox. Focusing too much on one aspect will create negative effects, however, using them in concert creates a balance similar to yin and yang. This relationship is the nature of the paradox and what makes it of such value to our lives when considering the impact it can have on positioning us to solve our problems. It isn't about being overly grateful or overly unsatisfied. There is a right and wrong way to use the Gratitude Paradox and it is centered in the two following aspects of its existence:

> *The Gratitude Paradox should be considered in the context of ourselves and how we affect our own life and problems, not things that are out of our control i.e. other people.*

> *Not being satisfied should not be the result of wanting more, it should be the result of wanting better.*

It is important to remember that this paradox is in the context of our own unique lives. Our challenges and experiences; not others. If we consider this in the sense of an intimate relationship, it is imperative to remain grateful for that relationship while understanding that it can be improved. We should not seek to change our partner but to reflect on ourselves and how we can improve ourselves and the relationship with the other person. If we were to think about never being satisfied in the context of our significant other, we're saying that they or the relationship isn't good enough. In the framework of the paradox, however, we acknowledge the value of the relationship, which commits us to always improving that relationship, and places the focus on what we can do to affect that experience.

It isn't about thinking that fault lies in another person or situation outside of us or trying to change someone else to align to what our view of who they should be. By doing that, you're taking your perception, which has already attracted problems, and saying that you have the appropriate view of who a person should be and/or how they should achieve that. That spells mishaps for the entire relationship where a better course of action is to change your own perspective and work on you. In the context of the paradox, we understand that:

> We love who our partner is, what they do, and the relationship that we have with them; and

> We realize that we can find ways to make that relationship more rewarding for ourselves and our significant other through our own self-development.

There is a common misconception that never being satisfied is the same as wanting more. In the this framework, never being satisfied means always wanting better. Better experiences, better relationships, and even better problems. There is a striking difference between the two, which can be exampled by the relationship between quantity versus quality. More is not always better; in fact it can actually be harmful. Too much of a good thing can be very bad. The wrong way to have a lack of satisfaction is by asking for more from life; the right way is by asking for better from it and from ourselves.

With our challenges, we shouldn't want more solutions, we should seek better ones. If we are struggling with having money, we shouldn't want more money; we should seek money of a higher quality. The type of money that comes with knowledge of use and discipline of saving or investing attached to it. That is better money; it carries its own personality because instead of just being more, it came with a lesson. I was first exposed to the difference between the two when I entered college.

Two of my graduation gifts were money from my father and money from my uncle. My father gave me $1,000 in loose cash and my uncle gave me a one-thousand dollar check and said that it had to go towards an investment or a certificate of deposit. With no direction for the cash, it was soon spent on nothing of significance. However, I kept the check for a few months thinking about where I would invest it, before ultimately depositing it in and donating it to fund a student skiing trip for a campus organization. While I didn't use the money for the intended reason that my uncle expected me to, the difference from the money my father gave me was striking. Better money. There are many situations which fit the need to be considered as better instead of more.

Perspectives

"Remember this maxim: When you change the way you look at things, the things you look at change. The way you perceive things is an extremely powerful tool that will allow you to fully bring the power of intention into your life."

- Wayne W. Dyer

After graduating high school my best friend, Preston told me that he wasn't out to change the world. He said "we all live in different worlds. Who am I to say that my vision of it is right or better than someone else's? The best that I can do is be the best me and hope that adds value." Faced with graduation and pressures of "what will I do" or "who will I become," Preston changed his perspective to reflect something more conducive to his future than worry.

He redefined what his own benchmark of progress really was; he didn't encapsulate it in some vision to change the world. He carved it out in his own psyche and laid forth the groundwork for creating his own future. He overcame what the problems of fear and insecurity were that were created by college applications, family legacies, and celebrity moguls. Preston positioned himself to create his own path in life and he did it by changing his perception. We can all use the power of perspective to improve our approach to our greatest problems.

8 | ACKNOWLEDGING OUR EXISTENCE

Introduction

The objective of acknowledging our existence serves as a primer to get our mind to operate from a perspective that is more helpful in solving problems. These acknowledgments seek to understand the specific reasons of why we are awesome and make us feel a little better about ourselves and our lives. This isn't meant to be an amazingly emotional (unless that's what you want or need) experience but it is supposed to be fun. It is meant to very clearly identify those things which make you a unique individual. Your talents, your passions, everything that you do or should appreciate about yourself. If you've been helpful to a friend, taken the time to ask someone how their day was, made an awesome meal one evening, or even just commented on someone's shoes today.

No matter how insignificant you may judge your actions, talents, personality, or character to be, the truth is that they matter. The more we begin to feel better about who we are and the lives we live, the better able we are to solve our problems and live happier lives. And we begin that process by thinking about all the ways in which we bring a little more awesomeness to the world. After having cultivated an understanding that we are worth it, we should get specific in acknowledging exactly who we are, why we are so special, and why we are worth living happier lives. Even if we already understand those points, it is always important to remind ourselves of how awesome we are.

Why You're Awesome

"Today you are you, that is truer than true. There is no one alive who is Youer than You."

- Dr. Seuss

Why are you awesome? Because you are, well you. That may seem a tad bit obvious but think about it. There is no one in the world who has had the exact same experiences as you. No one who thinks the way you do. No one who acts, sings…or doesn't sing, creates, laughs, and lives the way you do. You're different from every other person on the planet and every other Martian not yet discovered. And being different is a great thing. Heck, it's an - to risk sounding redundant - awesome thing because you bring something special and valuable to every table. Through your uniqueness, you have the ability to show the world a different perspective, a different joy, a different happiness, a different kindness, a different passion, a different creation, understanding, feeling; a different experience.

Because you digest information and occurrences uniquely, you can expose others to something that they would not have conceived of any other way. To be able to impact someone's life on that level is profound because we are all connected together in some way, shape, or form. And by influencing the life of one, you have influenced the lives of so many others. What you say, what you do, the value you bring is without a doubt special. And being able to contribute to people's lives in such a capacity is without overstatement. The reality that you exist is grounds enough to say "hey, I am special." And the fact that you are one in how many ever other people there are in this world is grounds to say it even more.

Without being different in some sense, what purpose would we have, what potential - none. But by being different, we are open to vastly ranging opportunities. It is like we're custom made for a life that we can customize. If I know one thing from life, it is that customization reigns supreme. It is of the highest quality, artisanal, beautiful, perfect. Unable to be replicated, we are absolutely unique. And if we could be replicated, we wouldn't be special at all - we'd just be regular and eh. But we're not, the only thing we are regular at is being special and being special is - I say again - awesome.

Another reason we are so amazing is because of our potential. It's unlimited which means we have the ability to do some spectacular things in this world. If we didn't have great potential, we couldn't possibly be great people because we wouldn't have the ability to be great; we wouldn't have the potential! Our potential is what directs us. That invisible but permeating feeling and understanding that we can achieve certain things in life. We develop and grow our potential by learning. The more we learn, the more we are able to do and achieve. So yes, another reason why we are amazing and great is because we can be amazing and great. We have the ability to, so something in us is saying we are.

You don't give a child a piece of candy unless they have earned it somehow. That child didn't get that Snicker bar without earning it and we don't get unlimited potential by not being worthy of it. We are special and everything we do carries that essence with it. If we think to some of the most impactful books we've read or speeches we've heard, how many times have you recited a line from them to get you through a tough time? And how many times have you passed those words on to someone else to help them? The same concept that is true for the books we read and the speeches we listen to and anything that impacts us is true for the impact that we have on others. We never know how far our actions or words will go in their impact on other's lives. At a minimum, it is important to be cognizant of the fact that they will have an impact. Our potential through our actions will have an impact and that is such a phenomenal thing, just like us.

At the risk of sounding like a broken record on repeat in telling you how amazing you are, yet another reason is because people that we may have never even met go out of their ways to do great things for us. You don't have people doing awesome things for people if those people weren't awesome to do them for. Things like create the 90s Nickelodeon channel with Hey Arnold, CatDog, All That, Goosebumps, and more. Things like making albums; Purple Rain, Appetite for Destruction, Slippery When Wet, Thriller, True Blue, and more. Protesting for civil rights, equal rights, and all rights. Writing books; The Great Gatsby, To Kill a Mockingbird, Jane Eyre, The Hobbit, Les Miserables, and more. Composing; Guillame Dufay, Heirrich Isaac, William Lawes, Leopold Mozart, Johann Christian Bach,

Johann Strauss, and more. These people, who were amazing, did amazing things, that made our lives more amazing. And they did it for the art, for the passion, for the love, for the spirit of doing because we are all deserving of such wildly awesome experiences. While I feel I could comment more on how awesome you are, I think it is time for you to chime in.

Thank You

Write a thank you note to yourself. Be very specific and highlight at least three things you like about yourself. Comment specifically, on why you like those attributes. Show yourself some love and don't think of it as coming off cocky. Just be straightforward and honest in detailing the things you appreciate. In your note, make sure you include at least two things that you do that you think are special. Tying your shoes a different way, smiling funny, dancing when no one is looking, cooking, anything that is special to you. What do those things mean to you? Be appreciative of yourself and hone in on acknowledging who you are and what you like about you. Comment on some of the good and bad things that you have been through in your past or are going through right now. What did they teach you about yourself and how did they add value to your life? What do you hope to do in the future with the learning from those? What can you thank yourself for doing now that will help you out in your future, even if it is writing a thank you note to yourself? Nothing is insignificant. Thank yourself again. Conclude with a favorite quote. There's space below if you dare…

360

Think of at least two people and a maximum of five whom you are relatively close with and whose opinions you value. Let them know that you are looking to understand yourself a little better and ask them if they would mind answering a few questions about you. After asking the questions, make note of their answers. It isn't important to have a lot of people to ask, what is most important is the quality of the feedback. The information that your close contacts provide should be well thought out and show the value that you add to their lives and to the lives of others.

1. What three words would you use to describe my most endearing qualities?
2. What is something that I have helped you with in the past?
3. What do you see in me that you appreciate?
4. What is the greatest gift I have ever given you?

If someone were to say...

What would you want someone else to say if they were asked about what makes you a fun person? Would you want them to say that you were fun because you're always up for an adventure, because you're peaceful, because you're generous and always looking out for others? What would you want them to say? You don't have to ask them; just think deeply about what it is you might possibly bring to the table. And you don't have to think of anyone specific; just try and see what you would want most people to say about you. Take a good look at yourself and try to understand what it is that you would like other people to be saying about you. This isn't meant to foster an external sense of approval; it's meant to develop an internal understanding of how you wish to exist. This looks to acknowledge some of the attributes of yourself that you find particularly valuable.

If someone were to say:

1. What makes you a fun person to be around?
2. What makes you smile?
3. What about you makes them smile?
4. What makes you laugh?
5. What makes you fill with joy?
6. What makes you a comfortable person to be around?
7. What makes you a unique person to be around?
8. What makes you a special person to be around?
9. What makes you an enjoyable person to be around?

Wall of Fame

Everyone should have a wall of fame. A compilation of some of their most cherished wins. Chess tournaments, winning a monopoly game against a friend, helping your mother with her business, anything that was special. Here is your opportunity to create your own wall of fame; write down all of the accomplishments that are notable to you. Awards, speeches, conversations with people, no matter how insignificant you think others may judge them to be. Even if it is you convincing a friend to do try something they've never attempted before. That is a win.

Grateful

List all of the things you have to be grateful for.

P.s. - you are amazing because you have these things to be grateful for.

9 | SELF DISCOVERY

Introduction

The pages that follow are meant to uncover the truths about yourself by asking questions to understand why you are who you are. What do you want out of life? Do you have dreams? Do you have ambitions? What is important to you and how did you get to where you are today? There are so many questions to life and our own histories that approaching it can seem daunting. However, the process of continuous self-discovery is an extremely important piece of our existence. The more we understand ourselves, the better able we are to create the lives we desire. The best way to discover ourselves is by asking questions that help us understand different aspects of our lives.

Our dreams, reasons for living, reactions to situations, habits, thought patterns, fears, loves, and more. Thinking about our lives from different contexts helps us to develop a broader view of ourselves. The questions we ask should be probing, digging deep and finding out information that may have been hidden from open view. The only way that self-discovery will have benefits on our lives is if we are honest with ourselves in answering these questions. This depth of understanding helps to create our futures, showing us how to carve out the paths we need instead of the ones we think we want, or that others have carved out for us. No matter how comfortable we are with ourselves, this is meant to get us more comfortable with deeper levels of self-discovery.

If you could sit down with your 15-year old self, what would you tell them?

There are things that you know now that you weren't aware of when you were younger. What things do you wish you knew then to help you out with some current struggle, to understand something about a person, anything? Maybe you wish you knew the importance of diligent work. Maybe you wish that you would have been educated on the importance of interpersonal skills. Do realize the importance of reading now and wish it was something you would have spent more time doing while you were younger and had more time? This question is meant to get you to understand things that you've come to see as important that could have yielded positive results for your life. Are they still applicable - are you doing them now? Are you reading more or is it something that you may tell yourself you should be doing years down the road?

This question is also meant to explore what is valuable to you? Do you find money important and wish that you had been told to invest in a stock when you were fifteen? Do you find relationships important and wish that you had shared more moments with you dad? What about time, did you waste a lot? The question isn't meant to evoke regretful emotions, but rather, create understanding and position you to think about the future. What are the things that you could be doing right now that will be useful for you later? Do you realize that one day, you may be asking this question again and would want to acknowledge things that you are currently doing that have been helpful? There are many things that we can spend our time doing; it is important to consider if we are investing it wisely.

What did you do as a child that you wish you still did today? What did you do as a child that you still do today?

Many of the experiences that you loved as a child were things that made you feel alive and purposeful. Why did you stop?! You can still translate them into happy and worthwhile experiences now. Sure, we can't all go outside and chase the ice cream truck but we can set aside some special time to indulge in sweet treats. There are many ways to recreate some of the most positive experiences we've ever had that existed during our childhood.

The reason for this question is to get us more connected with such youthful and invigorating experiences. We may not be able to go to recess but we can definitely take a break in the day to play or exercise. This question encourages you to think about what things were fun and what things can still be. Beyond the things that you may not still do today, what types of childhood experiences do you still have? How do they make you feel? Maybe you have been able to recreate your childhood through your children. In what ways have you been able to continue your youthful nature?

If the people who raised you walked a mile in your shoes, what would they be upset about that they taught you?

This question is meant to encourage you to consider what attributes you derived from your guardians that may make them feel ashamed. The different types of behaviors that you carry may be indicative of something deeply profound about your life. Maybe you smoke excessively and have learned to do so because your parents smoked. Perhaps you don't smoke and over exert yourself by exercising because your parents did smoke and you saw the negative consequences on their life. Our guardians can teach us through their actions in many different ways. We can choose to continue certain behaviors that they themselves engaged in. We can even choose to do the opposite because certain actions left a bad taste in our mouths. This question also attempts to encourage you to consider what your guardians may have taught you that would make them proud. Maybe you take the time to hold doors open for people because you saw your parents do so. Perhaps you make sure to greet everyone you pass to make their day brighter. You might even dance randomly when you feel good since your mother did. All of these things that they may be proud or ashamed of get us to question where we learned certain behaviors from. It also attempts to question what a mile in your shoes is like? Is it a good mile, a bad mile, a fun mile, a weird mile?

What is a strange or extremely personal and private occurrence you have experienced? Who did you tell about it?

This question is really meant to identify your trust centers. Who do you share your strange and perhaps most personal experiences with? Is it just yourself - why? Maybe you have secrets that are strictly yours. Do you just trust yourself or are you afraid to tell others? Maybe you have found that there is there no reason to tell others? Perhaps you just forgot what that experience was; who would you tell if you remembered? What makes that person, group of people, or even that pet so special? What do you see in them that you can trust? Have they been a friend for a long time? Maybe you have no one else to tell. For the people you can tell, do you think that you could learn from their personality types to attract more people of that caliber into your life? If you don't feel like there are people you could tell, do you think you should have those types of people in your life? Would you feel different if you had more people that you could trust?

What was the most agonizing hour of your life?

Do you know pain? What it looks like? What it feels like? How do you react under that pain? Was it controllable? Could you have prevented it from occurring? Why did you have to experience it? Did going through it potentially traumatize you from other things that were similar? This question is meant to encourage the consideration of each of these. Understanding your most agonizing moment of your life informs you about some of your tendencies by identifying a very emotional moment. To know what has created the pain in your life is just as important as knowing what has created your pleasure. For the latter, it may be possible to, in some sense replicate those pleasurable experiences and increase your happiness in life. For the former, it may be possible to stay away from painful situations or understand them more to alleviate any traumas that may have resulted.

I have a friend whose most agonizing moment in his life occurred when he was a child. He was chased down by a massive dog which inevitably caught up to him. The dog jumped on him and towered over him barking loudly in his face until it was pulled off. That experience created a lasting fear of any type of dog that my friend comes into contact with. Ever since then, he has spent more time focusing on the experiences about dogs and animals that have been negative i.e. mailmen being chased and bitten, owners and kids being attacked, etc. more so than the positive experiences. This information bias has solidified his fear against dogs. Once he understands his childhood event in isolation, he may be able to begin overcoming that pain and have healthier relationships with dogs. This will only occur through repetition to break the habits that have been routed in pain. But the first step is to ask what that most agonizing moment was.

Have you forgiven yourself for past personal failures? Why or why not?

Beyond understanding if you have forgiven yourself for past failures, this question is meant to clarify your perspective of what failure is. Was something a failure because it didn't play out the way you wanted or because something very bad happened? The question is also meant to enable you to define what forgiveness is. In movies, forgiveness is a topic that is highlighted a lot. A person who has committed some terrible deed, either by accident or on purpose must come to forgive themselves. Throughout the entire film, they go through experiences that deepen their understanding of the event. Finally, at the end of the movie, there is an "aha moment." The lights go down and there is a tranquil scene as you see the character forgive themselves. What that moment really is, is understanding. The character understands their inability to change the past and acknowledges that all they have is right now to make changes that will affect their future. Forgiveness is rooted in understanding, so what is it that you may not have forgiven yourself for yet? What else do you need to understand to begin that process and move ahead in life?

What is one dream of yours that you've temporarily pushed aside in pursuing? Why?

There was once a young man on a spiritual journey trekking across a vast landscape towards a mountain. Upon reaching the base of the mountain, he would meet a yogi who would question the insights of his travels. Two weeks into his voyage, as he walked through a village, he finally saw the formation of the mountain off in the distance. He observed an old woman crouched down in her garden and asked her how long it would be until he reached the mountain. The woman continued tending to her garden and did not respond. He asked again, "how long until I reach the mountain?" She said nothing and continued in the garden without acknowledging his presence. Frustrated, the man began to walk off. As he walked, the woman stood up and said, "two days, it will take you two days to reach the mountain." He turned around and asked why she didn't tell him that when he asked. She responded, "You asked the question while you were standing. I had to see how fast your pace was, how determined your walk."

Like the mountain, we will only reach our dreams if we go after them. How soon we achieve our dreams depends on our conviction and commitment. How determined are you to achieve your dreams? What are you doing right now that is taking priority over them, and ultimately your own happiness. We can find ourselves unhappy with life because deep inside, we know that we aren't doing what we want to do. We know that we aren't living fulfilled lives. We might be stuck in a dead end job, interacting with less than supportive people, and feeling like life is against us. Doing these things that we don't want to do, the things that we know aren't fulfilling and guiding us towards our dreams can create problems. Small dilemmas emerge that become large and inhibit our ability to live into our ever expanding potential.

So what are you compelled to achieve in your life that isn't being fulfilled? Why aren't you doing it? If something is a dream of yours, you should invest time in it in some notable capacity. Life wasn't meant to be wasted by doing things that don't speak to our purpose. Sure there are things that we may not feel like doing that we have to get over and just complete the tasks, but those things should be a *part* of fulfilling your life; not the majority of the whole. What this question seeks to answer, among other things, is whether or not what you are doing in your day-to-day life is really helping you to achieve your dreams. That's something that no one should have to live without. It also looks to answer if you even have dreams. Dreams have become, in a sense, a cliché phenomenon. However, that doesn't detract from the fact that they are important. So, what are yours? What are the thoughts about your future that may keep you up at night? What are those thoughts that make you smile? What are those experiences that, when you think about them, your problems of the moment seem to go away? We should all have dreams and work towards those dreams. If we don't, what are we doing? Really, what are you doing with your life that is more important than your purpose? Maybe your dream won't pay the bills. Maybe your dreams aren't feasible. Anything that prevents us from going after our dreams is an excuse. The difference between those who make their dreams a reality versus those who live unfulfilled lives is that the latter thinks that life happens to them. The former knows that they happen to life and that if they want their dreams to come true, they have it within their own abilities to make them. The same is true for each of us; we can't put our dreams on the back-burner. If your dream is to write a best-selling book and you're taking care of your parent on your deathbed and waiting tables to pay the bills, there is a way. Even if your dream is to write a book about your life, you have to be willing to use every chance you have to write that book. Maybe that is studying writing composition, reading to understand different authorship styles, or writing a paragraph a day. There is a way and dreams don't deserve to get put aside. They need you as much as you need them. Imagine if your dreams put you on hold. How would you feel? What would you be going through to tell your dreams, "hey, we're in this together" or "let's get this shit done!" This question looks to see what you are being called towards that should be in some way integrated into your life? Even if it is just one of your dreams, it is still a dream and it deserves your attention.

If you could choose your own life obstacles, would you keep the ones you have? Which ones would you keep?

This question gives you complete control of the challenges you face. It allows you to take a deep look at which obstacles have been more rewarding versus those which have been complete struggles. By asking this question, you acknowledge that there is a such thing as good problems. That there are obstacles you can learn from. This understanding is extremely important because if we think deeply, we see that all of our problems do hold some type of value. The question encourages you to think about what you may have learned from certain obstacles; that without them, perhaps you wouldn't be the same person. It essentially transforms your problems into opportunities and asks which lessons have been more or less rewarding. It makes you question who you are. Have some of your obstacles and their experiences been responsible for a key part of your character or personality? What in your adversity has been a good thing? What in it has been a truly unfavorable thing? This questions encourages you to consider if the grass really is greener on the other side. What would life be like if you could choose to have no problems? Would you still be the same person? Are your problems more valuable than you give them credit for being? This question is about showing people that their challenges are important to who they are. Whatever they may be, they yield positive benefits if we can only see through the temporary discomfort. With hindsight bias we tend to view problems as good experiences. Maybe we can shorten that process when experiencing challenges and understand that one day, we will look back at our problems and realize they were not as bad as we originally perceived them to be

What would you do differently if you knew nobody would judge you?

This question essentially asks about your freedom. What are you holding back because of other people's perceptions of you? Are you living your life or into someone else's expectations? Is it worth it? Who are you trying to please? Maybe you are trying to please your parents and become the doctor, lawyer, architect, or painter they were. Maybe you are trying to please your family by having a "better" career than your sister or brother. You may even be trying to please your college professor or best friend or family legacy. Why? Really, what are the reasons for doing so and do they make sense? We typically find ourselves trying to please others and in some sense, afraid to do what we want to even if we know it will make us happy or fulfilled or even just less stressed. Things like dance around the office because the culture is too rigid, smile at everyone you see, or even cut off talking to people for the first few hours of the day so you can focus. It all deprives us of doing what we want and what we sort of know we should be doing. If you're going to spend your life trying to please other people, you might as well change your name because you aren't you. You are living someone else's life. The world needs you; we already have that someone else. As Will Smith otherwise known as the Fresh Prince of Bel-Air said to Ashley:

> Will: Just because your dad likes something, doesn't mean you have to like it. He likes being a lawyer. You don't have to be a lawyer.
> Ashley: I *am* going to be a lawyer.
> Will: Ash, the world does not need another Philip Banks. In fact, we might not have enough farmland to support the one we have. No, the world needs an Ashley Banks.

What guilty pleasures do you enjoy too much to give up? Why?

Do you find pleasure in something that you hide away from your friends or family because they will find you weird, awkward, or different? Why? The truth is that they probably hide something they find pleasurable away from you too. And if they don't, they might be holding back on doing something they want because it would appear socially unacceptable. You don't have to be afraid of what you find happiness in. That doesn't mean that you have to tell the entire world either. It just means that one place that you should feel comfortable is in your own skin. In one of my past business courses, the professor told the class, "the nicher, the richer." What he was getting at was that the more niche focused, or specifically focused a product is, the better. This was because it was tailored to a specific audience instead of everyone in the world and because of that, you could essentially command a higher price. While that example was used in business, it has application here as well. You are not the only one who indulges in whatever you find pleasure in. You should feel comfortable in your guilty pleasures, whether you want to keep them to yourself because the fact that they are yours means something, or you want to share them for other people to know or potentially engage in themselves.

An additional benefit of this question is that it considers our relative levels of exposure. What guilty pleasures of yours are guilty because they might be considered slightly taboo? Eating snails is weird to some people, but if you travel to France, you will find that escargot is a delicacy. At one point in history, sex was widely viewed as a purely sacred act, only to be shared between married couples. For the most part, people who had sex out of wedlock felt guilty and wrong and could be socially ostracized. Where are we now - in a society where the view largely held is that sex can also be a recreational act. It is no longer something that people find as much guilt in as before. By whose standards do you find your pleasures guilty? Maybe you just need a little more exposure to what is 'out there.' What are you holding back that is unique to you? Do you stop yourself from enjoying your guilty pleasures because you find them weird? Why do you find them weird - is it because of how others will view you? Whose expectations are you living into? Could your guilty pleasures, if you didn't hold them back lead to something potentially liberating? Where we should be concerned about our guilty pleasures is if they create health concerns or harm other people. For instance, if you eat a piece of chocolate every time you hear your name said out in public. That's very dangerous if your name is Karen and a "My Name is Karen" convention happens to be taking place in your city. In all, this question seeks to identify exactly why some of the things you enjoy are guilty and if they really should be.

What is the most insightful thing you have learned about yourself this past year?

This question has multiple implications:

It creates an opportunity to identify what aspects if yourself need further development. Maybe you have learned that you have trouble with completing things. You've never been able to finish projects that you start; building models, reading books, creating plans, etc. That is valuable information that you can use to correct that problem. If that is what you've learned about yourself, then you can now assess that area of your life and improve it.

It considers whether or not your experiences are adding value to your life. Perhaps you have found that you spend a significant amount of time with people who have not been helpful for you or your development. Maybe each time you go out with your friends, the time is spent bashing others, gossiping, or talking about negative experiences. You may see that the time you spend could be better utilized with more like-minded people or doing different activities such as reading, writing, or painting.

It attempts to uncover where in your past, there is information that can help your future. For example, what if you learn that you are a lot stronger than you thought you were when it comes to dealing with stress? Perhaps you reflect on your life and recognize that you have been through very volatile situations but you've emerged and are continuing to live your life. That is highly useful information that can assist you the next time a particularly stressful situation arises. You can reflect on how strong you were and what made you that strong, which decreases the amount of energy wasted stressing.

Our ability to reflect is crucial and should not be underestimated. It fosters growth in the discovery of ourselves. Asking what we have learned that is insightful about our individual self helps us grow. It helps us identify something deep within that is strengthening. This aspect of self-discovery tries to keep us on the right track of making sure that we are engaging in experiences that support our growth and happiness.

We tend not to question what we can learn from our most recent experiences. We need this reflection. We need to take the time to consider the experiences we have been through and the role those experiences have played in our lives. The self-discovery process is one that unfolds as we grow older and wiser. Questioning what we have learned about our individual lives is the first step in that process.

What are the most rational fears you have? Why are they rational? Who would think that they are irrational?

When I was younger, I watched the movie *Arachnophobia*. I have been afraid of spiders ever sense. It isn't that I think every spider is some adaptation of a South American arachnid that if it bit me, I would die in a few seconds. However, I do stray away from them for what I view as a very rational fear that they may bite and that they are weird. Despite that, I recognize that my fear has been rooted in a lack of understanding of spiders. Particularly the fact that they are probably more afraid of me than I am of them. Or the fact that they prey on insects that are more dangerous to humans such as flies that carry diseases. If I were to go to an Arachnologist, they would view my fear of spiders as very irrational. They know something that I don't know about those spiders that potentially, if I did know, I wouldn't fear. This question seeks to consider what your fears are and change the perspective on who else would view them as fears. It enables you to think about fear in the context of relativity; if someone else could consider your fear as irrational, could you learn something from them? Why do you think your fear is rational in the first place? What have you been through that shows you that your fear is rational? This question is meant to educate you on the roots of certain fears, uncovering why you may face those fears.

If everyone in the world hated you, what would you do?

Could you imagine what life would be like if everyone hated you? If the barista spits in your coffee every morning? If people gave you disgusting looks and cynical comments followed you like a shadow? If your family absolutely despised you. Literally, if everyone hated your very existence. This question is meant to foster an understanding of your own self resolve. Is what you would do if everyone in the world hated you, what you should do? Does it matter if everyone in the world hated you? Could you still live happily? Would they stop you from doing what you want? This question is also meant to highlight the importance of relationships. No person is alone and we need positive, healthy relationships to thrive. They are a fundamental part of our existence. With everyone in the world hating you, it may make you feel like you were alone. Would you try to change their minds?! Would you not care and just live your life? Regardless, everything we do in life involves others and it is important to build relationships that aren't rooted in hate but in love.

> No man is an island,
> Entire of itself,
> Every man is a piece of the continent,
> A part of the main.
> If a clod be washed away by the sea,
> Europe is the less.
> As well as if a promontory were.
> As well as if a manor of thy friend's
> Or of thine own were:
> Any man's death diminishes me,
> Because I am involved in mankind,
> And therefore never send to know for whom the bell tolls;
> It tolls for thee.
>
> - For Whom The Bell Tolls by John Donne

This question encourages you to think about what you would you do if you existed but were simply alone in the world. What could you possibly do, what should you do?

If the people you are closest to, took a weeklong vacation through your mind; your thoughts, fantasies, fears, passions, etc., what would they come back saying?

This question is meant to identify what you constantly think about. Do you have positive thoughts where people would come back energized? Do you have negative thoughts where people would come back depressed? Or maybe you have thoughts that are neutral? Our thoughts play a significant role in the lives we lead because they determine our outlook on life and our reactions to situations. Perhaps your thoughts may have a larger role in how you typically feel throughout the week.

This question is also meant to identify the people that you consider yourself the closest with? What would they think about your thoughts and what would they come back saying? Maybe you have thoughts that they would want to encourage. Maybe you have thoughts that they would want to help you with. This question encourages you to consider what other people think about your dreams and fantasies. How would they perceive you and do you feel like their perception would be accurate? Would any of them think of you differently; for better or for worse? What if you took a vacation through their minds; would you think of them differently? Why or why not?

This question attempts to inform your authentic self? Are you showing people a different side of you than who you really are or the things you consistently think about? Should you? Are you being genuine? Should you be? Are you happy with how you portray yourself? Why or why not?

This question is also designed to identify varying degrees of like-mindedness in your closest circle. Of the people that you are closest with, which of their beliefs are in line with yours? Which are completely opposite? This isn't to say that if you aren't surrounded with completely like-minded people that it is a bad thing. The important thing is to understand where influences of thoughts might be derived from. Are you constantly thinking of your hopes and dreams? Who else do you know that has similar thought patterns? How helpful has your relationship with them been to your development? Should you spend more time with them or less?

If you taught a class and each student was you at a previous age, what would you teach if you had to teach the same subject to each student i.e. if you are 30; there are 29 students in the class ranging from ages 1-29? What one thing do you teach to all of them in one day?

Maybe you teach the class about the importance of exposing themselves to new ideas because you find it so important. Maybe you teach the class about people skills because it's something you wish you would have been better at. Whatever you decide to teach the class, it should be information that you view as extremely important. So important that you would have wanted it to be taught to you all throughout your life. This question seeks to question if you are doing something right now that is crucially important to you. Is the information that you would teach indicative of the life you are leading now? Do you find that information so important that you will continue to need it in the future? What is it about the information you would teach that is so important and what impact does it have or has it had on your life?

If you had the opportunity to get a message across to a everyone in the world, what would your message be?

What is important to you; so important that you need to get it out to the entire world? Across the landscapes of over seven billion people? In every country, every home, every hotel and motel. From every impoverished city to the wealthiest of nations. A message to babies who can't speak or understand a word of any language yet to the most educated and well-read of persons. To people in every religion to those who don't believe in a higher power. Even aliens and their friends whether they ride in space ships or reside in a different galaxy. If you had the chance to tell the world anything, what would it be? Would you tell them to have fun? Would you tell them that everything will be okay? Would you tell them to read, to play, to laugh? What information from you should the world hear? Something that you feel with your deepest conviction that needs to be heard, that needs to be said. What would you shout out to the world saying? Maybe your message is humorous. Maybe it is calm and tranquil. It might be uplifting. Maybe it is cynical or sarcastic. It could be neutral. But what is it? What is your message?

This question encourages you to consider your purpose? If you had a message to tell the world, are you telling it? Is that message so important that you should be telling it to the world? Your message is something that you know everyone should hear. It should make you think about what is important to you in terms of your impact. It should make you think about what you are or should be doing with your time and/or talents. Why are you here and are you doing what you should to live a fulfilling life? If not, why? And how could you?

Do you hold any convictions that you would be willing to live for?

Many questions tend to ask what people are willing to die for and they miss the importance of the things that we could potentially be living for. After all, living is probably a better way to use your time than dying is. It calls to question; what are you doing right now and is it worth the rest of your life? What things stir up a sense of purpose within you and should be given more attention? What do you feel compelled to do and are you doing it? Would you live for telling the people of the world that they are beautiful? Would you live for creating sustainable energy sources? Would you live for managing client money and making sure a family legacy is preserved? Or for educating students? What are you willing to live for?! It is a simple question but its answer deserves intense consideration. A lot of us know what we would die for.

We would die for a brother on his deathbed to take his place. But would we live for that same brother, to preserve his memory or extend his impact? Maybe we ask what we would die for because we know we don't really have that option. Maybe somewhere deep down we know that answering that question is a cop out because all it really does is make us feel like we would go to the ends of the earth for someone to show us what they mean to us. But to live for something requires more because we can actually do it. We know that the choice to die for something isn't typically a probable option, but it sounds good. It's a good sound bite. Living for something is real. It takes work and can actually be accomplished. For instance, in the movie, "The Dark Knight Rises," the joker promised the city of Gotham that for each night that Batman refused to turn himself in, people would die. As the death toll rose, the district attorney Harvey Dent falsely claimed himself to be Batman and turned himself in while Bruce Wayne (the real Batman) watched. Had Bruce Wayne turned himself in, it would have been suicide. His reputation would have been ruined and more importantly, Batman would have been gone forever. At the time that Harvey Dent turned himself in, Alfred and Rachel were watching on the television. Rachel became infuriated with Bruce for letting Harvey take the fall. Alfred responded: "Perhaps both Bruce and Mr. Dent believe that Batman stands for something more potent than the whims of a terrorist, Ms. Dawes. Even if everyone hates him for it, that's a sacrifice he's making. He's not being a hero. He's being something more." Batman didn't need to die for Gotham, he needed to live for it. And we need to identify what we will live for as well.

10 | EARTHQUAKE

Introduction

Problems are like earthquakes. A shift occurs; plates move and set forth an unstoppable trajectory of after-effects. In our lives, our shift may be a failed relationship, an irresponsible purchase, a self-serving action, the list goes on. And from there, the effects ripple. We develop an insecurity, continue buying things, or get comfortable with doing things only for our own good. Pretty soon, our effects have outgrown us and started affecting others in more ways than one. The damage presses beyond us and can even extend into other generations, like the effects our parents may have had on us.

They shake the very foundation of existence itself and affect other things far beyond its initial radius. This section of this book is intended to map out the process for solving some of our most significant problems and invite more happiness into our lives. It follows a five-step framework that places primary emphasis the implications of our past experiences. This framework has had positive benefits in my life and I am confident that it can have positive benefits in yours as well.

The first question that I had to ask myself was simple, "what are my problems?" What were the problematic situations that I was currently experiencing? For me, it was an easy question to answer because it felt like all of my problems were falling down on my life at once. That isn't always the case though. It can be hard to pinpoint problems because life is going so well or because we really feel that we don't have that many. In any case, we have to ask ourselves this question.

My list of problems looked like this:

1. I was $12,000 in credit card debt
2. My bank account was in overdraft every few months
3. My gas was turned off, which meant I had no heat, no warm showers, and no way to cook food
4. I was spending crazy amounts of money on my credit card, eating, drinking, and partying
5. I couldn't afford to pay for my upcoming senior year in college
6. Another business that I had been involved in launching was failing
7. I was having poor relationships with my parents, especially when I would visit them back home
8. I was going through a breakup with my girlfriend
9. I needed to end a relationships with one of my close friends in my life
10. I felt insecure sexually

When considering what my problems were, it was important to clearly identify the ones that were repeating themselves; problems that I had in some capacity, experienced before. I didn't start out looking for which problems were repetitive. First and foremost, it was necessary to list all of my problems out then group them together in similar categories. When I took a second look to understand which of my challenges had shown up before, it helped me to see just how sneaky problems can be. They dress themselves as different scenarios and show up through different people. Mischievous little fuckers; often times they get you so caught up, so detached from reflection that seeing them is damn near impossible. Problems come in many variations that we must train ourselves to identify early on. Otherwise, we run the risk of always being in a purely reactive state to our external environments. And the more time we spend reacting, the less time we invest in living. And the less time we are living, the less time we have to be happy. When I considered my list in the context of repeat problems, I was able to see how much I was stifling myself by approaching life experiences the same, time and time again.

My list of problems transformed into this:

Financial Management
I had faced financial challenge before. While my load of credit card debt was new, the feeling of financial burden was not. I decided to group all of the financial challenges into one category of Financial Management.

Business Experiences
Ever since I was thirteen, I had been trying to start my own businesses. A home cleaning company, a consulting firm, entertainment companies in high school, clothing lines, an investment company, and more. They all failed.

Parental Relationships
I constantly argued with my parents, which was very much rooted in criticizing them for not changing as people, not keeping up with the times. I blamed my father for our financial situation and my mother was just outright annoying with her tendencies.

Intimate Relationships
I had been with my girlfriend on and off for three years. We had broken up before about five times prior and here I was going through it again.

Friend Relationships
I was facing having to let one of my close friends go. Our relationship had reached a point where it just wasn't healthy for either of us to continue as friends. This had occurred with three other friends at different stages of my life.

The original list shortened because I realized not every problem I was experiencing was a repetitive one. While not having heat was a first time experience, it was a product of broader challenges that were financial and those were repetitive. In the case of not finding previous examples of problems, I realized that those challenges were more symptomatic than indicative of a recurring problem. For instance, one problem on my initial list was that I was spending crazy amounts of money on my new credit card eating, drinking, and partying. While this was related to financial management, it was also related to a problem of constant drunkenness with an extreme lack of awareness. It was an experience that I had to classify in a category of its own. Because it wasn't repetitive in a long-term sense (it happened weekend after weekend for a span of about ten months), I realized that it was a symptomatic problem.

Trying to stop behaviors like those directly would be the same as taking Tylenol® for a headache. It simply suppresses the pain out of view, it doesn't cure anything. Those non-recurring problems, however, still hint at something deeper - especially if they are more psychological in nature. For example, my sexual insecurity was something that I realized hinted at a deeper problem in my life. The feelings of insecurity would only arise when other problems in my life would feel like they were all pressing down on me at the same time. As my repetitive problems would emerge, I would feel helpless, unable to escape. I would begin to project criticism towards myself and others.

Criticism stems from comparison and amid my challenges, I would spend time comparing multiple facets of my life to others. Money, intelligence, sexual ability, personal & professional networks, etcetera, etcetera. These comparisons are where various insecurities would stem from. I would inflate certain ones such as my sexual ability by comparing my size, stamina, and knowledge to others. It wasn't until I realized that my sexual insecurity stemmed from the concentration of other problems in my life and that each one of those insecurities could be put to rest by understanding them, did I start to overcome them.

Size
Humanity has a case of the huges. Bigger cars, bigger houses, bigger dicks, and bigger tits. Seeing lavishly large cars, magnificent homes on television, and huge breasts and asses in porn. We tend to associate bigger with being better and one environment where ironically, it holds less weight is in sex. Relative to your partner(s), shape is actually a more fundamental indicator of pleasure than size. The matching of partner's respective packages is a stronger determinant of pleasure than a man being "large" or a woman being "tight." As cliché as it sounds, it really is all relative.

It is true that no person's sexual performance ability, whether male or female can be captured in one metric. That is as difficult as trying to value a car based simply on its color. There are very distinct components, yet they are all related and associated to each other. This is something that I had to learn so as not to compare myself or aspects of myself to others and really focus on developing my own sexual competency to offer more pleasure. I also realized that sex is not so much a physical act as it is the combination of very psychological, social, and emotional experiences. Through understanding the roles that our minds, our society, and our emotions play in our intimate relationships, we can heighten the dynamics of sexual pleasure.

Stamina
This one was fairly easy to overcome my feelings of inadequacy. I had only had one partner and as the age old adage goes, practice makes perfect[3].

Knowledge
For a period in my life, I was surrounded by people in which sex was a topic of conversation the vast majority of the time. This girl, that girl. The reality was that people would talk about their sexual wins and never their sexual losses. They never talked about their failures or things they had learned. Perhaps they didn't have those moments. What I realized was that I was comparing myself to people who had much more experience than I and was in conversations that were very ego-driven and biased.

The important thing for me was to make sure that I was seeking understanding and not excuses. My understanding carried with it the ability to take action. I could clearly identify why something was an insecurity, why it was invalid, and how I could change it. The flip side would have been to blame it on something out of my control, which would only stifle me. If I had stopped at considering the size of my penis as my only metric and not dived deeper, I would have been fabricating an excuse and not have recognized the depth of my insecurity. What I did to face these insecurities was educate myself, practice…and listen to more Prince.
As you know by now, I prioritize writing honest and open information void

[3] I also realized that my stamina increased when listening to Prince while engaged in the act.

of considering how my ego will feel afterwards. One of the reasons for that is because humanity has a tendency to be afraid of other people's perceptions and what others will think of them. I want you, as a reader to know, that there is nothing to be embarrassed about - so I commit to putting myself out there publicly. In the previous section, I asked the question, what guilty pleasures do you enjoy too much to give up? Here, we come full circle as I explain some of the guilty pleasures that I enjoyed to support overcoming my sexual insecurity in hopes that you too will be honest with yourself.

Education
I went on a reading spree, diving into as much information about pleasing the opposite sex as I could. Books were my primary source of insight, which informed me a great deal about some of the ill rooted perceptions of sexual intimacy as well as how to develop and strengthen my own abilities. It's interesting how broadening our mind beyond what we knew can create so much space for what there is to know and how false our assumptions can be. The greatest book that I read on this topic was *The Tao of Sexology*[4], in case you're looking to explore this avenue as well. The book offers value to both men and women.

Practice (TMI)
To keep this PG-18, I worked on getting some practice in. Real life practice as well as masturbation and a device called a Fleshlight® for stamina training purposes. I'll spare you the details.

Listening to Prince
This is fairly simple, I knew that when in the act, my mind would focus more so on the sexual energy from the music than what was going on down under. This helped me "distract" myself and be able to leverage that with or without the involvement of music. Music (specifically Prince) helped me learn how to properly focus when doing the do.

Analyzing my repetitive problems was a more iterative process than analyzing my symptomatic problems. I was required to become more reflective and to walk myself through the previous experiences in each

---

[4] The Tao of Sexology: The Book of Infinite Wisdom by Dr. Stephen T. Chang

category that I had faced multiple times before. To provide context, this is what those situations looked like.

Financial Management

Throughout a lot of my life, I had always experienced cycles of financial challenge. They differed in scope but it was always apparent that I had no clue how to manage my money properly. This was only further solidified and brought to the forefront of my attention when I experienced so many challenges at once. I've discussed the credit card debt and having no heat but in addition, a lot of my college life was spent either with a solid amount of money or with none to negative. There were many times where I cancelled lunches, dates, hanging out with friends, eating dinner, etc. because I didn't have any money. There were also many times where I did go out with friends, pay for dates, buy birthday gifts, eat out every night, etc. They were all in extremes; I always seemed to have an overabundance that I would spend through quickly or none that would keep me from socializing. In either case, I wasn't doing a good job in managing it.

Business Experiences

When I was thirteen, I launched my very first business. It was a home cleaning service and my first client was one of my mother's best friends. I went through her home, bringing my own cleaning supplies, scrubbing, sweeping, vacuuming, and cleaning every room in her house. When I finally finished, it was time to get paid. She asked me how much my services would cost and timid, I said twenty dollars secretly hoping she would offer me more. She didn't. When I was thirteen, I closed my very first business.

DZ Connect
The summer after I graduated high school, a neighborhood friend of mine, Chris and I decided to start a business. We would host parties for teens in the city and they would be the greatest parties ever. So, we designed a plan for how we would do it. We would incorporate, find a location, strike a deal with a venue to host multiple parties, hire a DJ, tell all of our friends about it, sell them tickets at the door, and buy an advertisement on the radio. But first, we needed money. My dad and my uncle pitched in $3,500 so we could rent out our first space. We had flyers made and literally tagged the

city. We put out a 30 second ad on the radio and got pumped! Saturday rolled around and the doors opened. People came in, many who we knew and many who we didn't. Riding on our fame, Chris and I were going to take our company, DZ Connect to the next level. We partied hard that night and so did everyone else. When the party finally ended, we went back to my house and counted up the cash: $1,700 in ticket sales.

We spent $2,500 to rent the event space, $600 on the radio ad, $150 on incorporating the business, $100 on the flyers, and $75 on miscellaneous items such as wristbands. We lost $1,725 on the event and only had $75 left over from money that was invested but not spent. With $1,800 now in our bank account, we spent the next two weeks hard at work being depressed. We didn't do much but hang out and talk about what we did wrong and lay in our own pity. After we finally stopped wallowing, we started to re-strategize. This wasn't like the cleaning business where I was just going to stop after one inkling of bad news. We found a new and cheaper venue that was in a poorer area of the city. It would invite a new target market but that was okay. Then, we decided on a theme for the party. There was a popular song out and we were going to capitalize on it. Went straight to ordering the flyers for the themed party. With a picture of the artist right on the flyer, people actually started thinking he would show up at the hole in the wall venue we rented out. The date was set and we got excited because on Saturday, we were going to make a comeback.

But on Friday, another group of people threw a party with the same branding. They found out about our party, contacted the venue and paid for a spot a day earlier than ours. The group was pretty well known in the area and they were trying to prevent us from taking any event money they thought belonged in their pockets. And they did; their party was a hit. With more money, more awareness, and one of the best DJ's in the city, we were out worked. I remember Chris and I would receive texts about their parties and get asked if we were coming. It was a slap in the face. When Saturday did finally roll around, we actually didn't have a bad turnout at the outset. But what we did have was a DJ who forgot the most important cord of his entire set up. The one that actually enabled the music that his machine was playing to be transferred to his speakers. He forgot his audio cable; the most precious connector. How was that possible?

Anyway, I digress. While Chris played damage control at the party, I rode out with the DJ. Thirty minutes out to his house to pick up his cable and then thirty minutes back. An hour at the outset of the party was wasted and everyone who drove by or stopped in to hear the music had left. For the latecomers, we were able to take in some ticket revenue but not very much. While we didn't go through another bout of depression, we did stop hosting the parties. We felt guilty that we couldn't pay my dad or my uncle back all of their money and to make matters worse, I realized that we wouldn't be able to pay them back any of it.

Chris and I both had check cards that were tied to our company account to pay for business expenses. One evening, Chris drove with a friend to Greensboro, which was about an hour and a half away from Charlotte. They spent some time with a few friends there and got back on the road going 100 miles per hour down the freeway. The only problem was that they were going in the wrong direction and actually ended up driving to Virginia. Chris's friend didn't have the money to pay for gas so he used the company account. $100 in gas money along with a few snack items. Our account went into overdraft and we were slammed with $35 overdraft charges per item. When it was all said and done, our bank account had a negative $265 in it, which my dad had to pay back to clear out the account and close it.

Katuffa
My sophomore year of college, I decided to launch a clothing company. I made the decision to do so the December preceding my winter term of classes. One of the reasons that I wanted to launch this company was to build something that my closest friends from home could begin building a financial legacy with. What that meant was that for Christmas, I sent them each a letter discussing the clothing line that I was launching and giving them shares of ownership in it. This way, by the time they graduated college, they would each have at least some capital to access regardless of their post-graduate plans. When I arrived back at school for the term, I was in execution mode.

I already had the designs for the clothes and began to reach out to suppliers through a platform called Alibaba. The only problem was that I couldn't start ordering samples until I had enough money. So until I went on my first co-op to save up do what I could with what I had. I purchased a web domain and started building out a generic site for the company that I decided to call Katuffa after hearing the name in class by a professor. When Spring came around, I started collaborating with two other individuals on campus for marketing. We created a campaign, bought marketing collateral, etc., etc. I was able to buy samples of clothes from China and have them shipped to my apartment. Two of my friends modeled while another took photos in the summer for the upcoming Fall collection. Finally, we had a site up, some initial inventory, and a marketing campaign. We were ready to launch at the outset of the Fall season. And that's exactly what we did.

The website launched, we sent email blasts, post cards, had wristbands branded, and more. We pushed the clothes out hard that month. A few weeks later, we had no sales. Literally, zero. I didn't find myself in the same type of depression that I had with DZ Connect but I did put Katuffa completely aside to work on another company that I was launching at that time and found more appealing.

The Board Investment Group, LLC

At the same time that I was launching Katuffa, I was also in the process of developing The Board Investment Group, LLC. Initially, The Board was a company that I wanted to start to bring African Americans on campus together and build something that would (like Katuffa) begin creating a financial legacy. It was to be something that in ten years would house some of the most powerful and influential African Americans. When I discussed this idea with my dad and my uncle, they made it very apparent that diversity rules. There was no need to silo it to African Americans but at the beginning, I didn't listen. I reached out to a few students on campus who reached out to a few more and we had a meeting to discuss what the company would look like and what we would do. Ideas ranged from creating a brokerage account to invest in publicly traded securities to hosting parties on campus to getting into real estate, etc. But we had to start somewhere and where we did start was with thirteen people investing three-hundred dollars each into a limited liability corporation. We were on our way. These thirteen members were the original founders and the only ones who retained ownership in the company. We began to bring on additional investors who were entitled to financial returns, however, no ownership stake.

The Board was set up into three primary divisions: Securities, Alternative Investments, and Real Estate. The Securities League was responsible for investing some of our assets into publicly traded companies. Alternative Investment's primary objective was to identify startup companies and act as a consultant to grow their business. Real Estate was charged with identifying exactly how we could tap into the real estate space to purchase property and grow our asset base. People would invest money quarterly and pretty soon, we began to grow. Each League had weekly meetings and we would all strategize on how to grow the business. Ancillary Leagues began to pop up; R&D, Branding, and Legal. More people began to invest into The Board Investment Group (B.I.G.) and it became bigger and bigger.

Pretty soon, there was no direction. We were doing so many things at so many times with no clear vision of where we were headed. We lacked knowledge in so many areas and I sucked as a leader. Unable to orient us in the right direction, I became very frustrated and confused. We were a year and a half into The Board with about $13,000 under management and two startups that we had invested capital into, and one consulting partnership with a new custom clothing venture. We were also a year and a half into B.I.G. becoming a stagnant investment company with twenty-six members, low morale and belief in the firm, and a great degree of disorganization. No one knew where we were going, people were missing meetings, emails went unread, and in some sense, The Board became a burden on people's lives.

I had failed again. This was probably the single greatest failure in business that I had ever had to date. It was one that really called me to question my inability as a leader and as an entrepreneur. I can't understate the amount of learning that I gained from it, however, that was not very clear when going through the process of trying to fight what was so clearly a failure from the start.

The Misfits

The misfits is a group of business failures that I tend to group into one because of their similarity in that their lives were so short-lived, however, they still hold relevance because they were indeed attempts at forging ahead as an entrepreneur. When I entered college as a freshman, my general business course was one of the best classes that I had ever taken. The book that we used wasn't necessarily new information but it was fun to engage with. When it came time for our first test, I had read through the chapters and found myself at the library helping a few other students study for the exam. They weren't grasping the information fully so I decided to go back to my dorm and write songs on the material that the book discussed. That writing turned into making music on and that music turned into raps. I made CD's for the students and gave them out. They said they helped so I kept on going. I made a CD for every business test my freshman year to help people retain the information that was in the text book. I must admit that because I wanted to make these songs fun, I decided to create the majority of them with a theme in mind that a lot of people in college could relate to - sex. So, with songs like Ratio Fellatio[5], discussing financial ratios like profit margin, I was off into the minds of students.

What these songs inspired me to do was to consider if music could be used to help out high school students as well. In high school, for a history project, I had created songs to detail the progression of Robber Barons. What I had the opportunity to do in college was to further that. So, I got my old history book from school and started writing. I went through a chapter on Slavery and began writing songs out. That would be used as my pilot CD. I ended up discussing the ideas with some high school students in Philadelphia and letting them listen to one of my songs made in college that wasn't sexual in nature. It was a hit and again, I decided to let additional people in on the potential earnings and sent letters along with shares of ownership in High School Hip Hop, LLC to my family. The only problem was making these songs took time, a lot more time than I had and I ended up not making any on for my High School pilot CD. What I did end up with was 70 songs on business that were used to study for tests.

Another one of the misfits was HSConsulting. This was a firm that I wanted to launch when I was about fourteen and had begun taking an

---

[5] https://www.dropbox.com/s/4fowo0wais1otk0/Ratio%20Fellatio.m4a

interest in stocks. What I did was take information from Yahoo! Finance and organized it into weekly or monthly reports on specific stocks that I thought people should invest into. I made business cards and a promotional brochure. I ended up having one client, my aunt who wanted to receive financial information and recommendations. I didn't know that I needed certifications at that time and pretty soon, the business had to be shut down.

The last band of misfits were Fresh Millennium Entertainment (the second coming of DZ Connect) and Savour Faire (the second coming of Katuffa). All in all, what is important about them all is that on a purely financial and existential basis, they are classified as failures. This happened eight times throughout the span of my life and it was definitely a problem that I considered to be challenging and one that needed to be fixed.

Parental Relationships

My Mother
My mom is very opinionated. It is her way...or her way; there is no other option. This was something that I had a huge problem with. When I went off to college, I was exposed to new ways of thinking, cultures, ideas, people, etc. It all had a profound effect on the way in which I viewed life. In a sense, there was a sort of rebellion against a lot of the things I had been taught growing up. Specifically, I was more confident in saying that I didn't like certain things (which my mother would take as being ungrateful), I liked to do things my way (which my mother viewed as me being rude), and I wasn't afraid to speak my mind (which my mother perceived as me 'being grown'). A lot of our issues revolved around the way that I presented my beliefs on certain subjects, which studying in the more direct/aggressive environment of Philadelphia, could have been approached differently.

It didn't matter at that time though; we would argue and I got sick of being called rude and for my mom to base winning an argument on who could yell the loudest. I was not a person who would yell; I preferred using logic and reason and my mom took that as me thinking I knew everything. We were on two separate pages and it became increasingly annoying. Every time I would visit home, I would impose my ways because they had worked for me. How dare my mother tell me to do something differently than what had created success in college. I didn't want to be treated like less than, because this view of being her son was something that I thought she needed to mature and that she needed to get unstuck from her ways and modalities of thought. This became a repetitive problem in the latter years of college when I would travel back home more. Every time, it was an argument and I couldn't break the cycle.

My Father
In college, my father and I clashed a lot. Much like the relationship with my mom, these clashes primarily occurred in the latter years of my studies. I remember the moment that was probably the most defining for those clashes, which ironically occurred freshman year. To provide context for that event and its after effects, you have to know that my dad and my brother did not have a good relationship at all and my dad's greatest fear was that he would lose having a good relationship with me as well. The characterization of their relationship is captured in the following story:

It was 2003 and my dad had just gotten remarried. He and his new wife brought my brother and I along with them to Jamaica for the first half of their honey moon. After a week, it was time for my brother and me to head back to the states. For some reason or another, he and my dad had a huge falling out while we were there. When we both arrived back home, he stole my step mom's car and drove two friends down to Atlanta where they went on an $8,000 shopping spree on my dad's company account. My brother and my dad's relationship was never the same after that.

That relationship is one that my dad did not want to repeat with me. I remember talking with my dad on the phone freshman year about how I wanted to transfer to Duke. I told him that I didn't like Drexel, the attitudes of the north, the culture, etc. He blasted me. He criticized how if I didn't think I could handle it, that I was being weak and probably should transfer. "If you don't think you can handle it, then maybe you're right. Maybe you should just transfer" reverberated through my brain in such a cynical tone. I began to cry and I told him that I needed to get off of the phone with him. I hung up and dropped to the floor and curled up in a ball feeling just like a baby. I was aware of the fear that my dad held for our relationship and subconsciously, I wanted him to feel the pain that I felt. And so I told myself right there that he had just ended that relationship, that he had just lost his only other opportunity at having a good relationship with his children.

While I fell back on that promise and continued in sometimes good and sometimes bad interactions with my dad, that event speaks to something that would continue to repeat itself. My dad's imposing views on me and criticisms of what I should do no matter how well I was doing in school. There was always his addition of how I should be living and how I should be carrying on, which made me feel like he was never pleased. Even though at times he said he was proud, it never felt real, and it was always after he had just said how I could improve or do this or that in addition. I grew tired of this and as his own financial and marital challenges grew tumultuous; I felt that he had no right to tell me how to exist because his own existence had no warrant for advice, direction, or insight. And this happened over and over and over again to the point where I wouldn't even argue; I'd just listen and become increasingly distant. It was a recurring problem.

Intimate Relationships

My first serious relationship was in college. Her name was Sydney. The way that I met this girl who I would ultimately date was the definition of serendipity. It was the summer vacation after my first year in college and I stayed in Philadelphia to mentor high school seniors who had been accepted into the university and were going through a preparation program. I lived a few blocks off campus with one of my professor's daughters, Amy, from freshman year. Her mother and I were very close and since we had become good friends, we decided to live together for the summer. It just so happened that one of the students in the preparation program was my roommate's younger sister, Katherine.

When Katherine came to campus for the program, she was scheduled to move into one of the freshman dorms. Her mother, Sydney, and I each helped her move her things into her new living space. While helping her move, we met her roommate who happened to be Sydney. Nothing of much significance occurred during the move in; however, Katherine and

Sydney became pretty close friends. They would go out and party together and a few times, when Amy and I threw a party at the apartment, they would join for a bit. At this time, I had made a conscious decision not to have a girlfriend and to spend my time focused on High School Hip Hop and class when it started back up again. That all fell to mush the more I interacted with Sydney. We would talk and ended up having a pretty good time together.

The tipping point was the text I received from Katherine one morning telling me that Sydney was interested. I asked for her number and we set up a lunch date. We met up, ate, talked, laughed, and had a really good time. From that moment on, I couldn't get enough of her. At the end of the program, she went back home to Jersey. We continued to text and talk late into the evenings. Sydney and I actually didn't start dating until the day she arrived back on campus as a full time student. I remember meeting up with her after she was all moved in and sitting on her bed telling her that I thought we should "go steady." And there I was with a girlfriend and a few moments later, there we were making out on her bed.

Over the next year, we had a blast. I was falling so fast and you could just tell that we we're enjoying ourselves. She was the woman who I gave my virginity to and the one who I constantly tried to surprise and shower with my affection. And the feeling was mutual; she exposed me to so much about living and was so pure and beautiful. She brought so much joy to my world. Pretty soon, our first year anniversary was on the horizon, which was also around the same time as her birthday. In preparation for both events, I did a little shopping. For her birthday, I purchased an iPad and for our anniversary, I planned out a helicopter trip around the city to show her how much she had elevated me and how much of a new world she had exposed me to.

At this time, she had just finished up her summer following freshman year and was moving into a new apartment on campus. I met up with her mother and sister, both whom I had met before and her father and uncle whom I had not. I walked in smiling, ready to be introduced to her father but there was no introduction so I said "hi, my name is David" and shook his hand. It wasn't a big deal; everyone was on the move trying to get furniture upstairs. Towards the end of the move-in process, Sydney, her mother, and I were all walking in the apartment building towards the elevators. Sydney's mom started to talk.

> Mom: "Sydney, guess what your dad just said when we were outside."
> Sydney: "What?"
> Mom: "Who's that man helping us with moving you in? I said David. Then your father said 'who's David?' I said that's Sydney's boyfriend. Then he said, 'Sydney has a boyfriend?'"

That moment hurt. and I felt that after a year of dating, I was at least warranted a "hey, dad, I have a boyfriend." I started to feel like she was trying to hide me or maybe that she didn't care about me the same way that I cared about her. After hearing that, I mentally checked out. I was stand offish and really just wanted to finish unloading furniture so I could go back home. And she could tell that my mood had changed. When I finished helping, I walked back to my apartment. Right as I was crossing a street, it hit me. This feeling of surrender, of defeat. At that moment, I physically felt my heart sink and I said to myself, "if she doesn't care about you, then why should you care about her?"

Later that day, it was time to exchange gifts. We met in a small garden area with a fountain and had the chance to talk about the conversation from earlier, but by that time it was too late for me. I told her that it didn't seem right that we had been dating for a year and her father hadn't even heard of me. I questioned why I hadn't come up in conversation once, not even between her mother and her father. It just wasn't something that she talked about with her father and I couldn't understand that. They didn't have that type of relationship and I held on to that feeling of inadequacy for a very long time. It became an underlying factor in two of our break ups that would come in the later months. I gave her the iPad but in guilt. I victimized myself by giving it to her and holding the thought in my head that she didn't deserve it. We never went on the helicopter ride.

A few months later in the fall, some very unfortunate events occurred. I was a part of a consulting course, in which our class was given $3,000 to work with Chevrolet to create a marketing campaign for their new

Chevrolet Cruze. We were competing against about thirty other universities. One of the requirements of the course was to host events that build awareness on campus for the cars. We were given access to three other vehicles to have on campus where students could get inside of them and check out their features. To preface our event, Fall in Philadelphia isn't necessarily the best time to have cars outside for students to check out. It's cold, windy, and tends to rain. This was no exception. We had four cars on campus on a blocked off street right in the middle of the central concentration of dorms. When it started to rain, we had to move the cars under an open area beneath one of the newer dorms. The space was large enough to keep all of the cars dry and offered enough space for a crowd of people to be under simultaneously. However, there weren't enough people coming outside to view the event and to win this competition for our class, we needed pictures of swaths of people. I received the bright idea to walk into a dorm and pull a fire alarm because I knew that if it was pulled, everyone from the dorm had to come outside and crowd under the driest area, which is exactly where our cars were. That would be prime photo capture time.

And that's exactly what happened. I called Sydney and asked if she could let me up, without telling her why. I went upstairs and hung out in the dorm for a few minutes. I told her what I planned to do and she did not approve, however, I was a little too big headed to listen. I stepped out into the hallway while she put her shoes on in her dorm to come and sign me out. And there it was; a bright red fire alarm. So, I did what any college student in an empty hallway would do. I started dancing and I 'fell' on the fire alarm. I let out a big grin as loads of people began to walk down the stairs and go out towards the cars. Pictures, pictures, pictures! The only problem was that a police officer overheard me talking about pulling the fire alarm with some of my classmates.

He tried to arrest me; however, my professor stepped in and prevented that from happening. Within a few months, I was being tried by our university conduct board. I pleaded not guilty and ended up having to write apology letters to the dorm and the fire department. I was required to pay $300 for having the fire squadrons come out under false pretenses. Throughout those months of interviewing with conduct officials and trying to preserve my freedom, I realized that I had lost my way. I felt so off and that I wasn't really myself and on top of it, my relationship with my dad was waning, and I felt burdened by life. And because of that, I told Sydney that we needed to end the relationship. She said she understood. A few days later, I found myself crying in her arms because I had let the only thing that was going right in my life, which was my relationship, go. And she took me back. Breakup number 1.

About five months later, I started my first co-op. I was getting extremely busy with Katuffa and The Board. The Board began to take up so much of my time that I was staying up late while having to wake up early the next morning for work. It was taking a toll on my life and I felt that something had to give. Again, I buckled under the pressures of life and told Sydney that I couldn't be in the relationship anymore. That was the first time that I had seen her cry and oh boy did it hurt. The next day at co-op, I found myself balling my eyes out in the bathroom. Tears fell into the toilet like raindrops. How could I hurt someone like that? How could I breakup with them and make them cry? I felt so guilty and after I wiped the tears from my eyes, I went to my computer and typed out an email to her explaining how I felt that I had made a mistake and that we needed to talk. That took a huge pressure off of me throughout the day and pretty soon, we found ourselves back in a relationship. And things went well for a while after that until I started classes again.

When I found myself back in class; it was the same story. There was a constant pressure to manage The Board and classes were taking a hold of my life. I was thrown again and something needed to give. This time though, she wasn't so understanding. We ended up breaking up and having a long conversation about our relationship one evening. We each wrote down the things that we thought had contributed to the breakup and talked through them. On her list was one thing that stood out more than anything. She talked about how I had never seemed the same or never been able to let go of the conversation that her mother and her had when she was moving into her apartment. That's when it hit me and I realized that I had subconsciously been holding on to that feeling for so long. I kept letting the relationship go because in holding on to that moment, I didn't think she cared so I would make her care about the relationship. She would feel the pain that I felt. It sounds so evil and that's what it was. When she brought that old experience up, again I found myself crying because at that moment, I understood that what I was holding against her was the fact that I thought that she didn't care. She didn't care about me after I put myself out there so much and told all of my family and friends about her. She was my first serious relationship, my first love much like my father's, and when I felt inadequate, I didn't know what to do. There was such a shift because after that moment when moving in, I stopped talking about her as much to family and friends. A lot of people didn't even know that I was in a relationship because I always held it in the back of my head that there's the potential this thing can end and I don't want other people to have the perception that I'm not available. I didn't cheat but I also wasn't proactive in letting people know that I had a girlfriend. I was so caught up in my own pain that I was creating destruction in my own relationship through indifference. I was withdrawn from the relationship. After having that conversation with her, we decided to take things slow but we were effectively back in a relationship.

The fourth time we broke up was when I was on my second co-op, had money to spend, and started exploring with going out and drinking. I didn't do much partying in my earlier years of college and when I had, it was all sober. And I dove into a new world full of drunken nights taking girls out on dates, and being wild. I felt like I didn't have any obligations pretty much. Sydney and I would still talk and were still friends but it was clear that we weren't dating. She took the opportunity to go on a few dates herself and talk to other guys as well. And that was fine. I obviously felt jealous about some of these and this constant repetitive thought about another man pleasing her (particularly sexually) drove my feelings of inferiority. Regardless, we talked through both of our experiences. I said that there really was no one like her and she informed me of the same.

However, that wasn't enough. I wrote to her in a little notebook about all of the things about our relationship that I missed, all of the things that I wanted to do, and how I wanted to be back with her. I dropped it off to her and told her to give it some thought. However, even that wasn't enough. I was at a friend's apartment when she texted me telling me to check my mailbox. I caught a cab back to the apartment and read the notebook. She said that she couldn't say she didn't want those things as well but that we weren't getting back together. I basically went crazy. That same day, she drove home to go and talk to a friend and I decided to catch a train out to where she lived in New Jersey. I called her in the train station and I am pretty sure I looked like a crazy person raising my voice on the phone telling her "no, you can't do this. You don't love me." etc. etc. I told her that I was catching a train to her and she said no, that it was crazy, and that this wasn't how people function. I hung up and turned my phone off.

I walked up to the platform and waited for the train. A few minutes before it arrived, I turned my phone back on and as I did, she was calling back. I had calmed down and I apologized. I told her that I was just upset and we agreed that we both were but that we would talk about it when she got back. We got off the phone and the train arrived. I got on, but not to go and see her, more so to relax my mind. I ended up going to eat and to watch a comedy show, which was ironic in that it was completely random and I sat next to a guy who told me about his own relationship struggles in college. The weirdest part was that his wife was next to him and he spent time telling me about how he missed the girl he fell in love with in college...who wasn't his wife. Regardless, Sydney and I ended up dating again and I threw myself back into it full force. This time, however, she was a little more reserved, which was understandable. I remember a time when she was taking a nap and my phone died and I needed to get in contact with one of my friends. I asked her if I could use her phone to message him through Twitter and she sleepily said yes. And that's exactly what I did...but I didn't stop there. For the first time in my life, I lost trust and also for the first time in my life, I checked her text messages.

One was between a guy that at the time, I really couldn't stand and who I had grown jealous of because I knew of his tendencies. The blurbs of messages that I focused on went like this:

Blurb 1
Guy I Couldn't Stand: "How are you and David?"
Sydney: "We're good, just taking it slow."
Guy I Couldn't Stand: "That's good. You know, I really like you all as a couple."

Blurb 2
Sydney: "Do you think guys and girls can be friends?"
Guy I Couldn't Stand: "What do you mean; without the thought of sex?"
Sydney: "Yes"
Guy I Couldn't Stand: "To be honest, no. I think that although they may be friends, that thought is going to come up."
Sydney: "I agree"

Blurb 3
I can't remember what 'Guy I Couldn't Stand' said, however, I remember Sydney's response.

Sydney: "You don't have to try to be on my mind"

So after seeing these, again, I surrendered. I thought we were good and I thought that we were working this out but having seen those messages, I gave up. This time, it became apparent rapidly. To be honest, I basically considered her as cheating on me and stopped caring about the relationship and whether or not it would be successful. That in itself led to me criticizing her, which was rooted in my own insecurities. I would constantly comment on how she could do *this* differently or do *that* differently and I drove her further and further away. There was one point where we were kissing and I held back. She asked me if I wanted to kiss and I shrugged my shoulders and said we could. She said "no, do *you* want to kiss?" I told her about how I didn't really like kissing because they were always wet ones. She got fed up and with good right. A few moments later, she said that she didn't want to continue this how we were because she didn't want to start holding a grudge or negative views of me. I said alright and walked out. What a strong woman! Not to want to view someone in a negative light and having the courage to cut off the relationship. I have to admit, it was a lot more courage than I had - just waiting for something to happen and being indifferent to it either way. Breakup number 5.

All of these breakups were a problem and it was one that needed to be fixed. I hadn't properly assessed why they kept occurring, however, the first step was to understand that these relationship challenges were recurring problems that warranted attention.

Friend Relationships

Daniel

My first experience in needing to let go of a close friend happened in middle school. His name was Daniel and we literally became best friends. However, Dan was a pretty bad influence. We ended up creating nicknames for people at school so they wouldn't know that we were talking about them in front of their face. It was such a bad thing to do. Matters only became worse; I began to play little pranks in class with Dan where we would use rubber bands to shoot off folded pieces of paper at people. My senses finally hit me and I realized that none of those activities were beneficial to neither myself nor others. If that's what our friendship was going to be like, I had a serious problem with it. I remember talking to my dad one day and telling him "you know dad, Daniel has really negative energy." Years later, I would find out that me saying that was one of my dad's proudest moments. However, I couldn't just end the friendship - we had history and more importantly, we were in the middle of a project for our math class.

We procrastinated on completing our project and when it came down to the wire, I was stuck with doing most of the work. Daniel had to come to my dad's office where my father actually ended up doing a lot of the work as well. It was one-sided and when it came to present the project, Daniel scored higher than me. I didn't understand how I was responsible for so much work and yet he received a higher grade than me. That was the last straw; I stopped talking to him. There was no warning; the next day I completely ignored him. It went on for weeks and our relationship was never the same. When we finally did communicate again, I was very detached and we were never really friends again.

Chris

We created DZ Connect together and spent a lot of time hanging out. While our time was really limited to the summer after my senior year, we were able to create a pretty tight bond. Chris was a player; on the basketball court and with women. Those were two things that he loved to interact with. He had dreams of becoming an NBA star but also spent a lot of time with girls. I must admit that he did practice playing basketball every day; he transferred schools to be able to start, and spent a lot of his time on the court. However, he also spent a lot of his time flirting and juggling between this girl and that girl…and that girl. He had women for days and I was astounded. Some would get mad at him while others fell in love. Still he always kept a few by his side. In order to handle basketball and the women, his grades suffered severely. He spent so much time doing what he liked; he missed out on doing what he needed to prime his future life. When Chris and I started DZ Connect, it was his first shot at becoming an entrepreneur and it was something that he fell in love with. While basketball suffered because school was out, he still placed a high priority on women. This was something that would continue to stifle Chris and because he hadn't done so well in school, it was almost like a way out. Basketball became a way out. Girls became a way out. DZ Connect became a way out because they were all indicative of something that he could achieve outside of being raised in the hood.

There were a lot of things that led to Chris and I to ending our friendship. However, the most impactful one was when he drove up to Virginia and put our bank account in overdraft. I remember waiting very long to receive the money as pay back but it never happened. That was something that I held on to for a very long time. Ironically, Chris was also someone who liked to hold on to the past a lot. He never really used it to create new solutions but rather to harp on old problems. It happened with girls, it happened with basketball failures, and it happened with DZ Connect. I stopped talking to him as much and whenever I would see him around the neighborhood, I would try to stray away or keep our conversations short. He would always mention how he missed the DZ Connect days and that we needed to hang out. I always agreed but never made any effort to meet with him. He lived right across the street and every time I would drive in; I would make sure to look out and see if he was on his porch so I could avoid him by acting like I was on the phone. Eventually, I went off to college and we stopped talking completely. I would occasionally see him when I traveled back home but it was never the same. I remember my junior year; I actually reached out to him and told him that I had held a grudge against him for so long. He had no clue. It was really just me holding on to something that in the end didn't even matter. But he was definitely someone that I needed to let go of.

Rich

I met Richard in my first general business course freshman year. Throughout the months following our introduction into college, we began to hang out more. I found myself going out to eat and study with Rich. Once, during the Winter term of our freshman year, when exams came around, I offered up my dorm room for him to stay in the night before an exam. Rich lived off campus with his parents and it was a little difficult commuting for an 8 am test. That invitation set a precedent that I found unfavorable for a lot of our future interactions. Throughout the year, I became increasingly busy with extracurricular activities and class. Rich started to impede on a lot of that time through extended conversations and unwelcomed visits. Back then, I really didn't have the courage to say "look man, please give me some space." I didn't want to be rude, however, his presence became increasingly so. He would carry on conversations well beyond the point that they needed to be and didn't seem to take body language hints to dial the conversation down. I also had a problem with him not having money. There were many times where I paid for his meals at the university cafeteria and when we would go out to lunch. He began to spend the night more, which really became a burden, particularly a hygienic one. I got pretty fed up and started distancing myself. I really didn't want to be associated with him and started brushing him off and cutting conversations short.

Rich started getting caught up in a lot of things that were questionable. While I've always been a fan of character over reputation, his reputation on campus became increasingly diluted. I experienced a few of those scenarios that contributed to that view, particularly on a financial side. A group of us went to a birthday celebration at a bar. One of my friends began purchasing shots for six specific people and Rich was not one of them. Despite that fact, he took a few of those shots and took part in eating food that was ordered. However, he left without contributing to any part of the bill. This happened again at a restaurant with a few friends where he collected everyone's cash and took it up to the register. He came back with change but all of it went into his pocket. No one realized until after we had all separated. There were multiple events similar to these and they only fortified the view that I had in my head of him being someone who used others. One of my friends said very clearly that he was the type of person who was trying to "keep up with the means of other people although he didn't necessarily have those means." He was trying to be something that he wasn't and that contributed heavily to the ending of our friendship.

Sydney
Sydney was introduced in an earlier chapter. At the time of writing this book, she was a friend (perhaps the longest lasting) that I realized I needed to let go of. I was becoming more of a hindrance to her than I was helping her. The same was true in the opposite direction. Our conversations were consistently on the topics of her relationships, however, year after year - there was no change, and I began to think that she wasn't really concerned with one. That in some sense, her struggles gave her pleasure. And I needed to let go; because the harsh reality of the relationship was that it wasn't healthy for either of us.

Conclusion

These were my repetitive problems. What are yours? After you've created a list, try to categorize them into segments. This helps to codify your challenges into more appropriate buckets as opposed frantically to trying to tackle every specific problem. It is important to remember that those smaller specific problems are really a part of a broader set of cyclical challenges.

After-Shock

What have the effects of your problems been on your life and on the lives of others? The problems speak for themselves; constant failed friendships and failed business, challenges with managing money, etc. Those were the issues; however, it was important to see what effects those actions were having on me in my personal life. I found myself stressed more and sleeping less to try to solve certain problems. I found myself partying more- to have fun and distract myself. All of these were symptoms from my existing problems and how I had been managing them. They were detrimental to my life because not only did they continue to grow, they perpetuated my repetitive problems. They were also having very nasty effects on the people around me. Not talking to my parents, criticizing my girlfriend, coming up short on bills at restaurants; these were all effects that were being created as a direct byproduct of my repetitive problems. They caused me to spend less time fixing my problems and more time compensating for them. When we begin getting symptomatic; showing increasing signs of being negatively affected by our problems, we start digressing. We misdirect our energy, which could be focused on breaking our cycles. The reasons for identifying the effects our problems have on us directly are twofold: to use as progress benchmarks as we break our negative cycles and to improve our health.

Progress Benchmarks

As I walked on the path of breaking my cycles, I found myself stressed less, focusing more, partying less, and with more quality (not over-consuming alcohol), acknowledging my former girlfriend, other friends, as well as my own traits, and being more confident in myself. That shows progress; problems that existed slowly became less relevant. I became happier, more full of life, more appreciative, and maintained higher levels of energy. These effects that your deeper problems have on you should be written down and crossed off of the list when they are no longer relevant - when they are insignificant to your progress. These accomplishments will be the basis for identifying specific areas in your life where you are clearly excelling. Acknowledge them.

Improving Health

More stress. Less sleep. Criticizing others. Over consuming alcohol. All of these had debilitating effects on my health, both mentally and physically. When you sleep less, there is no doubt that you will process situations differently than you would when your brain operates from a well-rested capacity. The same is true for criticizing others; you're really condemning some insecurity that you face and that isn't beneficial for your own mental health. The effects of my problems also extended into a physical realm. When I started my senior year of college, I was sick three times within the first six weeks of class. It is apparent that there is a direct correlation between problems and stress. The more problems we have, the more stressed we become. Higher levels of stress are strongly correlated to poorer health. This stress inhibits our immune systems, depresses our bodily functions, and decreases our energy levels and general satisfaction with life. As we alleviate the negative problems that affect our lives, we detach ourselves from these inhibiting factors and ultimately improve our well-being. I don't mean to say that being healthy makes you happier (in some cases, it does), however, having poor health can definitely make you unhappy and miserable.

The effects that my problems had on my life and the lives of others looked like this:

Effects from Financial Mis-management
- There were times I couldn't eat;
- There were times I would go out with friends and my card would get declined and someone else had to pick up the tab. I felt bad for them and for the friendship; and
- I would party and drink more, which obviously wasn't beneficial to my health.

Effects from Business Experiences
- I was losing sleep to manage an ailing business; and
- I experienced higher levels of stress.

Effects from Tense Parental Relationships

- I experienced higher levels of stress arguing with my parents; and
- I was criticizing my parents, which I am sure they did not like.

Effects of Tense Intimate Relationships
- I was criticizing trivial things about my girlfriend did that I didn't approve of; and
- I held personal insecurities of other guys.

Effects Challenging Friend Relationships
- I was stressed more trying to continue relationships that were clearly problematic; and
- I was relied on increasingly, to the point of sacrificing my own time to provide for others in ways that were neither beneficial to myself nor them.

11 | EPICENTER, MAGNITUDE, & FOCUS

Epicenter

Dogma: A belief or set of beliefs that is accepted by the members of a group without being questioned or doubted[6].

Imagine being a young child and each day after school, you come home to find your mother cooking dinner. She had every seasoning and herb available in the pantry and would shuffle through them depending on which meal she was making. Out of all of those options, there was only one that made it into every dish, Old Bay®. Whether it was to season fish, chicken, or even sometimes vegetables, that seasoning was always out on the table as she cooked. You noticed it, as it was the only thing consistent, the only thing repetitive in her cooking. As you grew up, you began to rely on the addition of Old Bay® into your own cooking. With every meal, it became a necessary ingredient. Your use of it became mechanical, almost instinctual and you never questioned it; it was something that simply became a part of the cooking aspect of your life. Through repetition, you became conditioned to think that Old Bay® earned a spot in every meal and you gave no consideration to whether or not that spot was truly warranted. It became embedded in your psyche; it became a part of you. It became something dogmatic.

Our lives mimic this, albeit on a greater scale. Our parents, our educators (whether academic or spiritual), our friends; they all play a part in our

---

[6] Merrimack Webster

conditioning. From such young age, they create solid impressions on our fluid mind states and become a part of our very being. Through repetition, they show us how to react to experiences and ultimately how to exist. We've been conditioned by the experiences of our past to carry ourselves in a very particular way and this way was cultivated through repeat actions. We learned how to react to virtually any situation; to the need to cook, to being afraid, to making financial decisions, to the death of a loved one, and so on. Those reactions created the paths for our lives, but like adding Old Bay® to every meal, we didn't always question the flavor of our reactions.

Our reactions are some of the greatest assets we have in life. Think to all of the stimuli we receive every day; alarm clocks, questions, comments, hungry stomach growls, traffic. The way we react to those various stimuli has a direct relationship to how we exist. If we choose to get up earlier to avoid traffic or to curse and shout at it. Those are reactions that have been taught and have become such a part of our being that we continue reacting the same way only strengthening the bond that our reactions, whether good or bad have on our lives. And we have to change that for the better. One of the most beautiful things about humanity is our ability to live vicariously through others.

Imagine: it is 1890. A man walks into a science lab where upon entering, dogs begin to salivate. Another man in the room, Russian scientist, Ivan Pavlov notices the dogs' behavior. For some reason, when Ivan's assistant walked into the lab, his dogs took that as a reason to salivate. So Ivan did an experiment. Each time he fed the dogs, he would ring a bell. Ding! Food. Ding! Food. Ding! Food. After a few iterations of this Ivan decided to ring the bell, however, this time, there would be no food. Ding! Nothing. But the dogs still salivated; they still expected that food to come. They had been conditioned to react to the stimuli of the bell with expectations of receiving food.

Humanity is in many ways conditioned like Pavlov's dogs. However, one way in which humanity is different is that we can use that experiment, we can use the experiences of others to change the ways in which we react. We don't have to wait for someone else to come along and re-condition us to react in ways more beneficial to our existence. We don't have to be shackled by the chains of our past, our partners, our friends, or our parents who have conditioned us to react in ways that may not always be so beneficial. Humanity can use the past to learn and construct its own future. But in order to do that, we have to identify where we learned our reactions from.

The first question that we had to ask ourselves in this process for breaking the cycles of repetitive problems that challenge our lives was "what problematic situations am I currently facing?" The question we have to ask now is "where did I learn how to approach these problematic situations from?" For me, this meant considering where I learned how to approach friendships from, where I learned how to approach parental relationships from, financial management and business from? I had to take the categories that characterized my repetitive problems and think about who or what in my life taught me how to manage them. It was never any singular cause, instead, where I learned how to approach my problematic situations from was always from multiple people. My brother, my mother, my father, an uncle, school, friends, and so forth. And that is okay because the better you understand the roles that different aspects of your history had on who you are today, the better able you are to break the cycles of that history that you don't want to stifle you tomorrow.

When you ask where you learned how to approach your problems from, you have to realize that you are providing yourself with something. It's something that you can't take back and it comes with a great deal of responsibility. It's also something that when you have it, you become void of excuses and you can't use what "was" as a crutch for what "will be." What you will be providing yourself with is freedom. Freedom works in two ways; the freedom from and the freedom to. When you ask yourself where you learned how to react to your problems, you are freeing yourself *from* the past. You are freeing yourself from the conditioning that has brought those problems into existence and impacted your life. At the same time, you are also freeing yourself *to* actively self-direct your life, expose yourself to new experiences, and to condition your own psyche to react in greater ways.

For the sake of consistency and perhaps even nomenclature, each person or thing that you consider as having a strong impact on the way you approach your repetitive problems should be considered 'Centers of Influence.' My problems and centers of influence looked like this:

Financial Management Centers of Influence
- Father
- Mother
- Uncle Oren
- Uncle Terrence
- Self-study (books)

Business Experiences Centers of Influence
- Father
- Self-study
- Media
- School

Parental Relationship Centers of Influence
- Father
- Brother
- My mother isn't included in this because both of her parents had passed by the time I was born. I only had past stories to gauge what their relationship was like but I also thought the learning from those was neither significant nor similar enough to consider.
- I also chose not to include a broad set of friends in this mix because after having considered my brother and the similarities of his early relationships with my parents to my current relationship with them, I could identify a strong correlation to my own repetitive challenges.

Intimate Relationship Centers of Influence
- Father
- Mother
  - I learned how to approach intimate relationships from my mother indirectly. She wasn't heavily involved with anyone while I was growing up but that lack of involvement also informed some of my own tendencies.

Friend Relationship Centers of Influence
- Father
- Mother

When listing out your centers of influence, it is extremely important to consider those that had the most pronounced effect on how you approach your problematic situations today. For instance, I learned how to approach friendships from a vast variety of places: the show Hey Arnold!, experiences with friends, my parents, and my brother. However, my parents had the most pronounced effects based on the quantity and depth of interactions that I saw with them. The way in which you identify those pronounced effects is up to your discretion.

Conclusion
So what are your centers of influence? Is it your parents, your brother, cousin, perhaps a school teacher? Maybe you learned how to approach certain problematic situations from television or books. There are many centers of influence in our lives and this question is meant to identify where they are.

Magnitude

Where have similar results existed among your centers of influence? Each center of influence that you have is responsible for varying degrees of how you approach certain problems. Maybe your sister has played a role in how you approach friendships, school, and work - key areas where you may have had problems. Her relationship to your problems warrants more attention being placed on understanding her in your approach to situations. This question required me to determine the degree to which I could track the problems I faced now with similar experiences among my centers of influence (Cofi's). The important thing here is gaining an understanding of relative magnitudes: the degree of influence from each Cofi. For example, my uncle Terrence was a Cofi that I learned how to approach financial management from; however, he was not instrumental in teaching me about neither friendships nor business. Therefore, his magnitude is smaller than that of my father's, whose influence expands throughout multiple areas. No one exists in this world alone, and our problems are not isolated simply to us. They are a dynamic unfolding of processes, created over time by habitual actions and reactions. What we have to realize is that our centers of influence may very well have contributed substantially to the way in which we act and react (I know I am beating a dead horse by now). The important thing to determine is *how much* of an influence they were. By understanding the magnitude that each Cofi displays, we learn how to focus our energy on breaking our cycles effectively. Doing this means we have to look at each problem and see where our Cofi had similar experiences.

Understanding Magnitude

Father
- Financial Management
    - My dad and I had strikingly similar experiences.
- Business Failures
    - Again, my dad and I had strikingly similar experiences.
- Parental Relationships
    - My dad was probably one of the best son's a mother could have. He has supported her for so long and treats her like a queen. On the flipside, there is one experience between my dad and his father that resembles our relationship today.
- Intimate Relationships
    - My dad and I had fairly similar experiences.
- Friend Relationships
    - My dad and I had strikingly similar experiences.

Mother
- Parental Relationships
    - I did not learn much from my mother about parental relationships; however, I have been told that she was sassy with her parents and others.
- Intimate Relationships
    - Growing up with my mother for most of my childhood, I learned a lot of positives about how to treat women. This wasn't necessarily about relationships but more so about respect, empathy, and understanding. However, I also learned how 'not to' be in a relationship, which was

something that contributed to my ability to be comfortable with breakups.
- Friend Relationships
  - My mother did not have similar friend challenges in her history. She has some really awesome friends and those relationships have lasted for a very long time. I learned a lot from her about how to have healthy friendships.

<u>Self-study/experience</u>
- Financial Management
- Business Failures
- Friend Relationships

<u>School</u>
- Financial Management
- Friend Relationships

<u>Uncle Oren</u>
- Financial Management
- Business Failures

<u>Uncle Terrence</u>
- Financial Management

<u>Brother</u>
- Parental Relationships
  - My brother and I had strikingly similar experiences.

<u>Media</u>
- Business Failures

My magnitude characterizations showed me that my father has had the greatest degree of influence on my life and my approach to problematic situations relative to any other Cofi. The high magnitude centers of influence are the ones that deserve the most attention. This meant that I really needed to gain an understanding of my father's own history to see why he faced certain challenges, which is the next step in the process for breaking the repetitive cycles that challenge our lives.

Focus

The question that we have to ask ourselves at this point is "why did my circles of influence with the greatest magnitudes experience *their* repetitive problems?" Here is where thinking in the aggregate comes into play. Take all of your Cofi's similar problematic experiences; analyze them, digest them, and assign specific examples of the issues in their time. Try to get a 360 degree view for why a center of influence experienced their problems.

For instance, my dad had a friend named Andre growing up who became like a brother to him. They partied together, fought together, survived together. They were family. As they grew older, their respective career paths diverged. Andre went on to take a variety of unfulfilling and dead end jobs and constantly struggled financially. My dad went to college and became an architect. As adults, my dad has helped Andre through financial situations only to find that cycle continuing in perpetuity. My father has always been there for him, extending his energy in vastly different ways with not much reciprocity. What I came to realize, growing up, was that Andre was a constant energy leak in my dad's life. He withdrew more time, money, and happiness than he produced. Sure, we all have relationships where we may extend ourselves and we give up more than we get. However, it wasn't about the constant dependency on my father. It was about the over-dependency, one that ultimately harmed Andre because he lost his sense of self, his own resolve and ability to overcome life challenging situations. My dad entertained this all throughout their relationships and he has never been able to let Andre go. Why? Because he views Andre as family and wants to be there for him to help, regardless of the situation or how many times it occurs.

He didn't realize that at one point in their relationship, Andre became over-dependent and my dad stopped helping him and began to hurt him. I understand the view of Andre as family; however, there are times when we must prevent ourselves from giving into even our family's whims. By not letting go of Andre, my dad was unable to let go of entertaining those attributes which prevented them both from growing. He will not cut off family completely, which I understand – however, it is possible to stop funding them, coaxing them, holding their hand and solidifying their grip into your time and energy.

This information is extremely useful on our own journeys as well. Without knowing that history of my father's, I would have never truly known why I continued to experience friendships that I constantly had to walk away from except for the fact that my dad faced the issue. With my dad, he constantly needed to walk away from one person whereas my experience has been away from multiple. The understanding about this problem in particular was that these people were extreme energy leaks. They built an over dependency on anything or anyone outside of themselves to bring some sense of joy, happiness, peace, or escape from life. My father and I have been unable or unwilling to decipher these types of people early on and understand the impact they will have on our lives. That has been detrimental. After considering the similar experiences in friendship that my dad had, I understood why he faced those experiences. I could approach my problem from a broader view and learn why I had those problems and difficulty in preventing them.

When you consider the past experiences of the Cofi's in your life with the greatest magnitudes, you will begin to understand why it is so important to consider the roles they played and what their impacts on your life have been, whether positive or negative. The benefits of this process are significant. Among them are (1) the opportunity to potentially help your own Cofi's to break their cycles, (2) to truly understand why you have been unable to break your own cycles, and finally (3) to break them and experience greater levels of happiness.

You are further removed from your Cofi's problems than they are and looking at their past experiences provides you with an outside look from an internal perspective i.e. you're looking at a problem in their life, a problem that you have firsthand experience with. You know that you have a repetitive challenge affecting your life and you know who you have learned how to deal with that challenge from. But you don't know what root of the problem is. It could have been your Cofi's inability to do something, surmount some fear, reconcile some relationship, etc. You don't know *why* they couldn't break the cycle, which upon learning will offer insight into why you have not been able to break the cycle.

The Analysis: Friend Relationships

- <u>The problem:</u> My dad needed to let go of a friend.
- <u>Specific Examples of Issues</u>
  - Sending Andre money
  - Experiencing stress with Andre's alcohol problem
- <u>Why he couldn't break his problem</u>: My dad viewed Andre as family and wanted to help him no matter what.
  - Family is one of the most important relationships in my dad's life. He grew up struggling with his brothers and sisters but despite that, they always supported each other. It is impossible for him to separate himself from his family, which he viewed Andre as a part of.
- <u>Dive deeper (why, really?)</u>: Andre built up an over dependency on my dad, which my dad couldn't recognize.
  - Had he been able to identify that personality trait early on, he may have been able to manage their relationship differently.

Self-Application

What I realized was that I faced the same challenge; identifying over dependent personalities. And because I like to help people, I failed to recognize the stifling affects I was having on other's lives when they would become overly dependent on my ability to listen to them, console them, acknowledge them, advise them, etc. I also failed to recognize the effects those relationships were having on my life as well, often times after the effects had already taken place. The way in which to solve that problem was to become better at identifying those overly dependent personalities. This would equip me with options. To remain being an acquaintance with a person as opposed to a friend, to encourage them to become self-dependent early on in the relationship, to run in the opposite direction of friendship completely, or some other action. Here is what this process of understanding how to break my repetitive problems looked like for my other challenges:

The Analysis: Financial Management

- <u>The problem</u>: My dad spent in extremes meaning when we had money, we spent it and when we didn't, we struggled.
- <u>Specific Examples of Issues</u>
    - Impulsive buying behaviors
    - Over-drafted accounts
    - Not being able to buy toys
    - Extravagant vacations followed by periods of no spending
- <u>Why he couldn't break his problem</u>: He had no consistency.
    - My dad never saved any money nor did he actively invest any income. He built a habitual dependence on big checks to come in from large architectural projects. When they did come in, times were good. When they didn't, times weren't so good.
- <u>Dive deeper (why, really?)</u>: My dad's childhood was rooted in extremes.
    - My dad's family didn't always have money, but when they did, they would use it. It was almost as if receiving money made them feel like they had to use it and experience it before they didn't have it again, which can create challenge.
    - Despite that, my dad was never able to break the cycle of spending money in extremes and missing the importance of having a consistent building process to grow his wealth.

Self-Application

What I realized was that I did the exact same things. I didn't save consistently, I didn't invest consistently, and I didn't even receive income consistently. In college, my income was literally dependent on my father's income and that was sporadic. Even more sporadic was how I managed my money. There was no telling when I would receive money the next time, which should have been grounds for me to save what I did have and build up a nice cushion. But I did not and I needed to re-condition myself to be more consistent with generating income as well as saving and investing it.

The Analysis: Business Failures

- <u>The problem</u>: My dad shuffled through business opportunities, never fully capturing the value from any particular one.
- <u>Specific Examples of Issues</u>
    - His architectural firm was failing.
    - He gave little energy to his art, which at one point was intended to be a business.
    - His daycare business partnership was failing.
- <u>Why he couldn't break his problem</u>: My dad never properly focused nor did he choose the right people to work with.
    - My dad was always on the move. His brain operates faster than any computer humanity will ever create. From this topic to that topic to that topic. He is always thinking about what is next and what will be. Doing that prevents him from actively pursuing any one opportunity. Even if that one opportunity will serve as a platform to open up other opportunities.
    - My dad also had a challenge with choosing the right people to work with. A lot of my dad's partners lacked accountability. A lot of his potential partners often times tried to get too far with too little i.e. they tried to get over on him and use his services before any money was paid out to him. Identifying and bringing on board the right people proved to be a challenge for my dad.
- <u>Dive deeper (why, really?)</u>: My dad grew up having to take what he could get.
    - When you grow up poor, you don't always think about long-term potential. You have to take what you can get and keep trying to move up the best way you can. You aren't worried about one thing, you're worried about six.
    - As a child, my dad moved from job to job, to grow and develop which worked then. It even worked for him in college. He never silo'd himself into one thing; he always sought to capture value from a wide variety of opportunities. However, as he grew older, it actually ended up stifling him when things like business weren't fully

flushed out enough. For example, my dad's brilliance in being able to see opportunities meant he would see two at once. Instead of starting one company that could grow, he saw the ability to start two companies that could grow and co-exist to help each other. However, the right amount of energy was never given to bringing those companies into existence nor did he determine if it was appropriate to only launch one at the outset. My dad was the type of person to launch them both.

Self-Application

I realized that I was spreading myself too thin. I was trying to launch multiple businesses at one time, take classes, work, uphold my responsibilities to extracurricular activities, etc. Spreading my energy across so many different things meant that one wasn't receiving enough attention. I never fully flushed out my ideas and just jumped into new businesses. That provided me with a lot of learning, which has been extremely beneficial. However, that learning wasn't always apparent when a business was failing. I also sucked at identifying the right people to work with. If I could better understand a person's character and work ethic early on, I could have saved myself a lot of headaches in business.

The Analysis: Parental Relationships

- The problem: My dad had a singular experience with his father that changed his perception of him. My brother had multiple experiences with our father that destroyed their relationship.
- Specific Examples of Issues
    - Dad
        - My grandfather borrowed money from my dad once that my dad had spent a long time saving. He never paid it back and it took my dad a long time to forgive his father.
    - Brother
        - My brother ran away from home.
        - My brother cut off his connection from father.

- Why they couldn't break their problem: They experienced an inability to forgive.
    - Dad
        - He couldn't come to forgive his father. My dad was so young and spent so much time saving up his money. He had an overwhelming sense of pride having saved it and when his dad asked for it but never repaid, it was like a shot to the heart.
    - Brother
        - He couldn't come to forgive our father. My brother felt less than in the eyes of my dad; unappreciated and unloved. He sought my father's approval in various aspects of his life and when he realized that he didn't see it in the way he wanted, he decided to cut my father out from his life.
- Dive deeper (why, really?): They couldn't separate their ego from their situations.
    - My dad and my brother became so caught up in their past experiences and the fact that something had happened to them, they never forgave their parents. Their egos had been bruised to such an extent, they became detached. Instead of forgiving their parents, they outcast them and held negative views that only grew with each 'bad thing' their parents did.

Self-Application

It took me a long time to forgive my father for his comments about being weak when I wanted to transfer to Duke. When I did forgive him, I had already latched on to other things about his personality and character that I held in a negative light. I gave him strife for it. My mother constantly criticized the things I did and I couldn't stand it. I never realized that she only did out of love and was only operating from ways of communicating that she was familiar with. Her family grew up arguing; that's how they communicated. They never communicated from a position of peace; whoever was the loudest was who won. I never let my ego go enough to understand the implications of either of neither my parent's history nor the beauty in their personalities. Had I done so, I would have eliminated a lot of the criticisms that I placed on them.

The Analysis: Intimate Relationships

- The problem: My dad had a woman who he fell madly in love with who broke up with him[7].
- Specific Examples of Issues
    - Dad
        - When my dad was in college, he dated a woman who he fell in love with. She broke up with him and he took it extremely hard.
- Why he couldn't break his problem: Prior to that, my dad never knew what love was.
    - Early on, my dad was exposed to women galore. Even in college, where the ratio was 10:1 and he and his roommate literally had to hide in their dorm and act like they weren't there when women would bang on their door. Experiencing love was something new, something different, something profound for my dad that he wasn't able to quickly recover from.
- Dive deeper (why, really?): My dad couldn't let go of neither the past nor his retaliation to it.
    - After breaking up, my dad did what I've seen a lot of men do. He became a little insecure and started approaching his relationships with women as more of a numbers game than a quality of interaction experience. He took that experience and held it against many of the women he would interact with after that.

Self-Application

I have a problem with taking one thing and blowing it out of proportion. This occurred with my girlfriend, whom my inability to understand her history and relationship with her father, stifled our relationship. I held something that was so rooted in ego against her for so long and it really

---

[7] Ironically, my brother did a similar thing.

messed up the relationship because I started finding more things to consider about her and our relationship that I disagreed with. It was my own insecurity that I needed to get over. I also needed to stop taking one experience and extrapolating its effects throughout my life.

All of this understanding was related to identifying why my centers of influence experienced similar repetitive problems. I must qualify this, however, by noting that breaking these cycles does not require an understanding of why a Cofi experienced them: that information may not be available or accessible. However, it does make solving problems much simpler and easier to manage. For example, I recognized that my friend, Marco faced issues that constantly repeated themselves. He over-exerted his own personal energy into people in his immediate network; supporting them financially, emotionally, and even spiritually. This led Marco to depend on substances like alcohol to distract himself from life's challenges. Where did it come from: his father died when he was very young, which forced him to become the man of the house.

His role became embedded into his psychology; he attracts and retains people like family and friends who depend on him, which drains his energy and overall satisfaction with life. His relationships cycle and problems with people repeat throughout different time periods. People become dependent and he detaches; wild emotions ensue, the relationship either dies or muddles along. If it dies, another person or in some cases an activity takes a pre-existing person's place. He wasn't taught how to have energy-enriching or sustaining relationships: with family, with friends, or with activities. His interactions end up burning him out and depriving him of increased levels of happiness. Marco never learned how to monitor, regulate, or grow his energy which continues to perpetuate itself in his life as his constant dependency on stress outlets grows. Now Marco's father may have experienced this same issue; but he doesn't have access to why. Despite that, one thing that Marco can look at is that after his father passed, he stepped up to the plate. He became the man and people identified him as the leader, solidifying his position as the go-to person when things went wrong. While Marco can continue to retain that role, he should continue to do it in a way that is healthier and encourages more of the people around him to generate higher levels of self-awareness and self-dependency.

Conclusion

The process for solving your repetitive problems requires you to ask yourself five questions:

1. What are your repetitive problems?
2. What have the effects of those problems been on yourself and others?
3. Where did you learn how to approach those problems from?
    a. Here, you will develop a sense of who your centers of influence have been and their roles in your current approach to life.
4. Where have similar results to your problems been in the lives of your centers of influence?
    a. Here, you will gain an understanding of the different magnitudes of influence that your centers of influence have had on your life.
5. Why did your centers of influence with the greatest similarities experience their repetitive problems?
    a. Here, you will understand why you and your centers of influence have been unable to break your repetitive challenges. This is the foundation for creating the solutions that will break those cycles.

The end result of this process is that you will gain an understanding of why you face the repetitive challenges you face and why you have not been able to break them. This is the diagnosis and now we need to look at what the remedy is and its positive side effects.

12 | THE FRAMEWORK

Introduction

On May 16, 1984, Prince released the song *When Doves Cry*. It a profound piece of work, which received critical acclaim and numerous accolades. It was beautiful, but its very beauty was rooted in anguish and pain. The song characterized the history of a child who had experienced trauma in his youth, a struggle that was translated into a groundbreaking piece of music. *When Doves Cry* was emblematic of the experiences so many of us have with our parents and the results those experiences have on our lives in future generations. Understanding those results can only be achieved through careful consideration of the past. We don't have to the perpetuate struggles and challenges that have brought themselves into existence under the radar of our own awareness.

We can excel beyond the cycles that challenge our lives and break free from the bonds that stifle our independence. Maybe you are like your father. Maybe you are like your mother. Maybe you're just like your cousin, sister, or brother. But that does not have to be your reality if you don't want it to be and more importantly, if it isn't beneficial to you. The final section of this book is meant to create the solutions for your repetitive problems. Everyone's will be different because of the inherent differences in each of our challenges. However, what follows should be used to create your own solutions, to take the process used in the preceding section and apply it to develop very tangible actions and break the cycles that pose problems in your life and inhibit your happiness. This is what it sounds like when doves...dance, smile, become happy, you decide.

The Framework

1. Refine Beliefs
2. Expand Centers of Influence
3. Set Goals
4. Build Reminders

The Framework

We've gained an understanding of why our repetitive challenges exist and now it is time to break those cycles. This begins with organizing those problems based on their root, results, and then finally the solutions framework.

Root
What was the underlying problem preventing you from breaking your cycle? This is what was you discovered when "diving deeper" in the previous section.

Results
Reiterate the effects that your problems have had on yourself and others. You will need to cross these off the list as you break your challenge cycles.

Solutions Framework

A four step process:

- Refine your beliefs
    - Recognize that you have to change the way you think about your problems! You can't keep approaching them the same way.
- Expand your Centers of Influence

- Get some exposure to different people, ideas, and ways of thinking in order to establish new goals that will help you break your challenge cycles.
- Set Goals
  - Many times, we find it difficult to create change because we lack an understanding of the direction we're headed. After you've expanded your centers of influence, start creating goals and living into them.
- Build Reminders
  - Living into your new goals can be a challenge and it's a huge help to create reminders. You have to develop new habits to reform your past behavioral patterns. Tell the people around you so they can help you. Maybe even carry around a notebook as a physical reminder.

Financial Management

- Root
  - I lacked consistency.
- Results
  - I didn't have money, was spending impulsively, and was living paycheck-to-paycheck. There were times I couldn't eat, times I would go out with friends and my card would get declined and someone else had to pick up the tab. I was partying and drinking more, which obviously wasn't beneficial to my health.

Solutions Framework
- Refine my beliefs.
  - If I didn't have consistent streams of income, I couldn't spend like I was. I would depend on quick fixes. The truth was, I wasn't going to win the lottery and didn't need to depend on money just appearing. Wealth is a process; it doesn't just happen. I needed to establish goals and actively work towards those goals paying no mind to

things that didn't align to them like other people's expectations.
- Expand my centers of influence
    - I needed to start exposing myself to different people who managed their money more successfully than I. Especially people who perhaps had similar experiences. I also needed to expose myself to different information; books, articles, videos, etc. that could assist in guiding me to create financial goals and live into those goals.
- Set goals
    - Either get a consistent source of income or spend in less extremes when I do receive money from my parents;
    - Cook more!;
    - Pay down debt;
    - Think long-term;
    - Save money; and
    - Invest money (when you have the discretionary assets available).
- Build reminders
    - I told my friends that I needed help staying true to my goals;
    - I kept a small notebook with me that I took EVERYWHERE to remind me to stay focused, especially when going out to a club, which prevented me from over-spending; and
    - I set up bank account notifications to keep my financial management at the forefront of my mind.

Business Experiences

- Root
    - I was spreading myself too thin;
    - Not fully flushing out ideas; and
    - Choosing the wrong people to work with.
- Results
    - Business failures.

Solutions Framework

- Refine my beliefs.
- I needed to focus on things that I should do instead of all of the things I could do. I needed to understand my own "why" for existing and never stray away from that. I also needed to invest unrelenting time on the things that supported that reason for existing.
- Expand my centers of influence
    - I needed to read more; particularly on things that informed my own existence and strategies for business. This ranged from books on self-awareness to corporate strategy. I also needed to expose myself to more students and adults who were successful entrepreneurs.
- Set goals
    - Determine what I wanted to be the best in the world at;
    - Invest my energy in thinking through my long-term impact;
    - Put people who I intend to work with through the ringer;
    - Find and interact with the right people (potential partners, mentors, etc.); and
    - Be patient and create plans for creating that impact.
- Build reminders
    - Read every day; and
    - Do something related to my long-term business vision every day.

Parental Relationships

- Root
    - I was unable to let go of my ego; and
    - I did not consider my parent's histories and ways of being brought up.
- Results
    - I wasn't going home much; I was arguing with my parents a lot and thinking about them in a bad light, which was highlighted by constant criticisms.

Solutions Framework
- Refine my beliefs.
    - I needed to let go of the thought that one experience with my parents should encourage me to look at them in a negative light. I should have viewed relationships as very dynamic processes that go through a wide variety of experiences; not things that are static. It is best to cultivate relationships and think about the value I can provide and things I can learn as opposed to things I can criticize.
- Expand my centers of influence
    - It became necessary to talk with people who had positive relationships with their parents; people who were able to accept differences and transcend their own egos. Everyone has challenges with parents at some point, but the people who can let go of those challenges for the sake of experiencing positive interactions are a special breed.
- Set goals
    - Acknowledge my parents regularly but spontaneously and genuinely;

- o   Ask my parents about notable stories about when they grew up; and
- o   Meditate to transcend my ego.
- Build reminders
    - o   Slap myself i.e. make it known in my journal that I wouldn't be here had it not been for my parents

Intimate Relationships

- Root
    - o   I was unable to let go of things, my ego outweighed the decisions that were right, and I stopped staying true to acknowledging my girlfriend.
- Results
    - o   I experienced multiple breakups and really lost a sense of myself.

Solutions Framework
- Refine my beliefs.
    - o   Relationships should be viewed as partnerships where people interact, acknowledge, and consider the beauty of each other and their unity consistently. I needed to let go of, like with my parents, singular 'bad' events being subconsciously embedded as a negative view of my partner and/or my relationship.
- Expand my centers of influence
    - o   Talk with married people. They have some of the best advice, particularly if they have experienced relationships in college. I also needed to reduce my talking time about girls, girls, girls, in the same ego-driven context with friends to maintain an appropriate level of respect for relationships.
- Set goals
    - o   Listen to more Prince (the degree of understanding of women the man has is insane);

- o Speak your mind about the value you see in EVERYONE (make acknowledging a normal part of your existence);
- o Learn about the woman's history (but leave some to exploring in a relationship);
- o Hold expectations primarily on yourself and not other people; and
- o Have fun! (lighten up, kid)
- Build reminders
  - o Keep a relationship notebook between the two of you that you write to each other in consistently.

Friend Relationships

- Root
  - o I couldn't recognize over-dependent personality types before getting into a relationship with them.
- Results
  - o I kept having to cut myself off from friendships with people, which increased my stress levels.

Solutions Framework
- Refine my beliefs.
  - o I can't be the only one providing value in a relationship and that is what the harsh reality of my past friendships had been. Friendships need to be mutual experiences of sharing, providing insight, and understanding. I needed to cultivate as opposed to just provide; it wasn't helpful for me nor my friends.
- Expand my centers of influence
  - o People who have had friends for very long times are great people to become friends with and to learn from. I also needed to start interacting with people who had developed a sense of self-dependency and awareness.
- Set goals

- - Learn how to identify over-dependent people early on.
- Build reminders
  - I chose not to build reminders in this situation since learning how to identify over-dependent people early on would provide me with the chance to consider the long-term trend of the relationship, which would serve as a reminder in itself.

These processes takes time; it is a process and should be approached as such. But the results will be well worth it. For one; I'm not stressing about my gas bill since that has been paid off. I am slowly paying off my credit card bill but was able to talk to the credit card company so they aren't calling me anymore. I must admit that sometimes I fall back into old ways but it's been good to have reminders like my friends and my notebook to keep me on track financially. I am single and working to develop myself and it feels great. One thing that I've done to help develop a sense of self is institute a daily practice called Power Hour. It consists of watching twenty minutes of the Fresh Prince of Bel-Air, twenty minutes of listening to Prince, and twenty minutes of meditation.

All of it helps to keep me focused and particularly on the meditation end, it keeps me aware of the beauty of life, my relationships, and humanity's existence. I also read every day and all of these things have helped, more than anything, to keep me aware. Aware of my goals, aware of my relationships, aware of my happiness. My life has experienced tremendous changes and my happiness has definitely grown. I never stopped loving life but I've never loved it this way. Of course I still face challenges but at the same time, those challenges are now facing me and their ability to fight has largely diminished.

13 | THE MATTHEW STORY

Matthew was one of the most interesting children that I have ever met in my life. The thing that strikes me the most is that I knew him for a total of less than one month if I were to group each of our interactions into one continuous stream, yet he had such a dynamic impact on my life and I hope yours as well. Those interactions educated me on how powerful early experiences can be in forming our perspectives on life. Not only do they have a profound effect on the way we view things, but consequently, how we interact with people, react to situations, and carry ourselves. The influence that our adolescence has on who we are today cannot be overstated. They inform such a substantial part of our existence that placing them into the context of our current successes and problems is paramount. My dealings with Matthew frightened me because I know that in his, what was then only twelve years of life, he had been stifled. Stifled by his mother, his grandmother, and his general environment. I have since lost contact with him; however, I hope that he is one day able to break the cycle that established itself in his life very early on. This is the Matthew story.

During my Freshman year attending Drexel University, I developed a routine of visiting the local community garden next to the dormitories on campus. The community garden was an extremely peaceful place. It was a square lot, with a mulch path cut diagonally across its opposing corners. On each side of the path, the garden was fenced in, forming two triangles. Each side was filled with fruits, vegetables, and flowers. There was a small fountain that I would typically listen to from the outside of the fence. The community garden was a place that I could go to relax and meditate.

My regular visits there proved to have substantial benefits for my life, especially when unexpected things happened. One weekend, as it was misting outside, I walked down the path and saw a young kid limping and dragging his jacket behind him on the ground. He looked extremely tired, like he was about to collapse. I ran over and asked if he was alright and he said that his body temperature was low. Thinking that he said blood sugar, I panicked and asked him where he was going. Feeling nervous for this kid's life, he said that he was headed home and pointed to a street sign that read Summer St. He dropped his jacket and kept walking. Still under the impression that this kid was about to pass out, I picked up his jacket and walked with him.

We made small talk; his name was Matthew and he had just come from the playground. The temperature dropped and when it started to mist, he decided to go home. His limping and dragging jacket on the ground, I came to realize was pure theatrics - something I would find he was very good at later on. Despite this, I asked him why he didn't just ride his bike to and from the playground and he said that he didn't have one. We reached his house within a few moments, he walked in, and I left. The experience was without a doubt a weird one. But the most interesting thing that I thought of was the fact that he didn't have a bike. With me coming from North Carolina, every kid had a bike. Later that evening, I went online and searched for one to purchase. Thanksgiving break was a few weeks away and I figured that I would drop the bike off as an anonymous present before going home for the holiday.

I continued to visit the community garden; it was after all a very peaceful place. As Fall fell to a close, exam time came around. After my finals, I decided to relax at the garden before going to pack up and go home. As luck would have it, I saw this kid Matthew in the garden running around by the remaining fruits, vegetables, and the fountain. He saw me and with a surprised look and ran away. I chuckled and got back to my meditating. A few minutes passed and he was back:

"Hey Matthew, how are you?" I said.

He said that he was doing well and then dove into a very involved and wildly vivid story. He told me that he was in the garden looking at the chickens and pointed towards a blue tent. I looked over but it looked like it was really just a tent protecting some vegetation from the impending cold weather. Then he started to talk about how he was the President of the garden. It was amusing so I entertained the conversation. His mother was the owner so that made him the President. And because he was the President, he could make the rules.

Rule # 1: There always had to be an open gate for him to enter.

Rule # 2: He was the king of the garden.[8]

His mother was also a secret spy who worked for President Obama. She had a private train that traveled to Washington D.C. and Peru directly under the community garden. There was a secret knock combination on one of the garden doors that would grant access to the underground train, but I wasn't allowed to know what that knock was. That was classified information and I dared not to intrude. Matthew then told me that he had been kidnapped before. This comment appeared out of thin air and I was taken aback. At that time, my thoughts were that Matthew had an extremely wild imagination. He was having fun and making things up, which seemed normal. There was nothing to it, but soon he went into details that made it difficult for me to think that it was just his imagination running wild. He said that when he was younger, he had in fact been kidnapped. The man who took him from his mother, told him to strip and that he would suck his genitals. His precise words were:

"He [the kidnapper] said, strip for me, strip for me, I'm going to suck your thingy thing."

That's when shit got real. He said that he had also been abused and his mother, too. It was the reason that his father wasn't allowed to see him anymore. Once, his dad was beating his mom and Matthew jumped in to stop him.

"No dad, don't hit her!"

His father slapped him to the ground. My mind was in a whirlwind; we

---

[8] I assumed it was possible to be the President and the king simultaneously.

went from chickens to underground trains to domestic abuse. What was real and what was fantasy? Even if only specific parts of the stories were true, it was enough to realize that something seriously wrong might have been going on at home. Later that day, I called my mom and my pastor to tell them the story. I asked if calling Child Protective Services was the appropriate course of action. They agreed.

When I called, I told a representative the story and she asked if I had seen any physical evidence of abuse. I hadn't; the only thing I could depend on were the verbal explanations from Matthew. She asked for his address: I didn't know it and was happy that I did not. If something abusive was not going on at his home, I didn't want to be the one responsible for Child Protective Services visiting, his mother getting upset, and starting to be intolerant and perhaps even lead to being abusive. The only information that I could give here was the street name. I doubt they ever followed up.

The bike I ordered for Matthew didn't arrive by the time I left for the Thanksgiving holiday. However, it was there when I came back to campus. So I decided to give it as a Christmas present before leaving school for winter vacation. With the weather changing, I began to visit the community garden less frequently and I didn't see Matthew for a while. The time ultimately arrived to go home for the winter and I needed to drop off the bike. As weird as I thought the situation was, it was even weirder that I walked to his house that evening to scope the scene out and make sure everyone was asleep before dropping the bike off. All of the lights in the house were turned off so I walked back to my dorm, wrapped up the bike, and asked a friend to help carry it over. We took the bike, dropped it off on the porch, and walked out of the front gate. As soon as we turned out of the fenced yard, a bald, body builder type man with a wife beater tank top and shorts on walked past us and into the house.

"Holy shit, that guy was huge. Was that his dad?!"

I never found out.

Winter vacation passed but the cold weather was still very pronounced. I fell back into my normal school habits, albeit, visiting the community garden less frequently. One evening, I was walking back from dinner at the university's cafeteria. Then it happened, Matthew came along riding on a bright red bike from Target.

"Nice bike, Matthew." I said. "Where'd you get it?"

His response: "Some crazy man put it on my porch."

And then it hit me. Yes, I was some crazy man, buying some kid a bike because in my childhood, everyone had a bike. This was the city, though, everything was in closer proximity - who needed a bike?! Plus, it was Philadelphia, no one gives random gifts in Killadelphia. What was I thinking? I quickly realized that Matthew had some serious issues in his life and that he could very easily talk or walk his way into a vast array of dangerous situations. Anything could happen to him the way he was able to freely venture wherever he wanted and whenever he wanted. If something were to happen to him, it would be me that people saw him with on multiple occasions and me that became a questionable person. And there I was, thinking to myself and saying "you need to remove yourself from this situation."

I told Matthew that I would see him later, never intending to. I would cut my visits to meditate at the garden to infrequent evening times. But then he asked me where I was going, and I said to my dorm. Big mistake. He said he would go with me and started following me on his bike. I told him not to, but to no avail. So I made a very vital decision - I kept walking.

I walked until I found a set of stairs attached to the back of another dorm that led up to a walkway. I ran up the stairs, knowing that he couldn't carry his bike up them. As I arrived at the top, he was still trying to get the bike up the first step. I darted off, and didn't look back. I arrived back at my dorm, sat down, and was hit with this feeling of disgust. How could I run away from some kid? Everyone in his life had probably run away from him. His father, his friends, anyone whom he had ever sought an interaction with. I promised myself that I would never run away from a child again. In telling my friends about that most recent experience with Matthew, we really began to question how bizarre everything had been. We all agreed that it was wild, but it wasn't yet over.

That winter was one of Philadelphia's most brutal. It snowed so much throughout January and February that classes were cancelled for the first time since the 1800s. It just so happened that on the one day I decided to lose discipline and visit the community garden, I saw Matthew again. He was making snow angels on the path that split the garden. He hopped up, picked his bag of Twizzlers® off of the ground and walked over.

When he made it over to where I was standing, he noticed that his shoes were untied. He asked me to hold his Twizzlers® while he tied them. As he began to tie his shoes, a student from the University began to walk past us. Matthew fell on the ground in front of him and started twitching and shaking wildly, as if he was having a seizure. He started to yell random fractions of words that sounded like gibberish. I apologized to the student for Matthew's behavior and he walked around us. I gave Matthew a disappointed look. He responded happily and excitedly with "that guy thought I was crazy" and then smiled. When I asked him why he did it, he shrugged his shoulders and said "I don't know." So I gave him his candy and started to walk away. Again, he said "that guy thought I was crazy" and he began to laugh. He laughed so hard in fact that he let one rip, he broke wind, he farted. Whatever you choose to call it; that's what it was. And even though that only added to his laugher, he managed to eek out one sentence. It was a sentence that I'll remember forever.

"Ooh, that was a wet one."

That was the moment when my pace of walking picked up. He touched the outside of his back pants pocket and put his hands towards me telling me to eat his poop. He started saying it louder and louder as I walked further and further away. "Eat my poop, here, eat my poop" with his hand extended outward and now following close behind me. "Eat my chocolate milkshake." Then I pulled a very shady move; one which I will always feel *slightly* ashamed of. I saw a friend, walked over to him, and told Matthew that my friend wanted to play with him. Then I walked away, leaving the two together. I thought it was a very appropriate course of action given the circumstances. My friend was confused, Matthew was undeterred, and he continued to follow me asking me to eat his poop. I had had enough. I tapped his hand, put my hand up to my face and said "there, I ate your poop, okay. Now what?" He paused for a moment, stuck his hand *in* the back of his pants, pulled it out and said "eat my –"

I broke my promise. I ran…again.

Spring arrived: a new season filled with new flowers and a fresh perspective. Now, I was adamant about not running into Matthew anymore. As fate would have it, I visited the community garden one Saturday while the temperature was warm. You think I would have learned my lesson by now. But no, there I was again, this time watching him shoot a BB gun at the door of the garden's fence. He kept shooting towards the door and trying to find a live animal like a bird or a squirrel (or a me) to lay waste upon. I watched as that gun slowly turned towards me. The duel was about to be on. My weapon: constant verbal iterations of "don't shoot me." His weapons: a BB gun, a trigger-happy finger, and some tiny little imaginary man or woman inside his head saying "shoot to kill, shoot to kill!"

And that is exactly what he did. He fired that BB gun with his tiny trigger happy finger and his comrade in his brain cheering him on. And I felt it. I felt that little pellet hit me square in the stomach and again, I walked away. This time, not to my dorm but to where a few friends were hanging out at a campus common area. Little did I know, Matthew followed me and had brought with him; in addition to his BB gun a stiff yellow plastic bat. I found out that he had followed me when I suddenly felt the bat whack me twice in the back. But that didn't matter; I was around other friends now who could witness this abuse. To think, I needed six college friends sitting outside talking to help me deal with a twelve year old. One of my friends (who was very sassy) took his bat and his gun and gave them to me while she scolded him.

I took his weapons, and with his mental confidants weeping in defeat, walked over to his house. I approached the porch and noticed that the front door was a Dutch door; split in half at its horizontal center. The top half was open and before I knocked on the lower half, I looked in; it was a pigsty. With junk everywhere, the house was ransacked and smelled like smoke. It looked like a house that the city would condemn because it wasn't safe to live in. It was difficult to see how he and his family could live there. But they did, and as I knocked, Matthew stood at the gate and stared at the ground, sad and defeated. His look seemed familiar to him, as though he had been defeated in his life before. And here I was another symbol of defeat in his life. His grandmother answered the door. I told her that he shot me and hit me with the bat. After giving her his weapons, she replied very nonchalantly, "Okay, thank you." She called Matthew over and in her soft and subtle voice, told him that he knew better. I walked off of the porch but I didn't walk alone. There was Matthew, back out and already prepared to wreak more havoc. I couldn't comprehend why he hadn't been reprimanded more severely. A timeout, a stern talking to, at least something more than "Now Matthew, you know not to do that." It was like she didn't believe or want to acknowledge what was very clearly a real situation. It was delusion and already affecting Matthew as a child. It was pitiful.

For a period of a few months following that, I didn't see Matthew. I also stopped going to the community garden completely. I did not expect that the next time I saw Matthew would be my last nor that it would provide me with a lot of insight about the "why" of his life. Why was he in such desperate need of attention and why did he grow so attached so quickly? The last time that I saw Matthew was when he was moving away. Like most of our previous encounters, it occurred near the community garden and by 'chance.' Oddly enough, I was walking by his house and he saw me. He walked over and told me that he was moving away. His mother was outside so I walked towards her and introduced myself. She looked no older than twenty-five: a heavyset woman who was very loud and very vocal.

She began to tell me about how she was studying at Temple and was a lawyer. She was moving into an amazing house with a three-car garage. She was also about to graduate. She iterated that she was finally about to experience a better life and that she was extremely happy. While I mean no disrespect to her level of competence, the way she spoke was very childlike. Her sentences were choppy and her words mispronounced; not the type of language you would not expect to hear from an attorney, particularly not when you first meet them. Despite the casual nature of the conversation, I was still shocked by her language. I wished her well and walked over to where Matthew was standing. He then proceeded to tell me that he was dying; that he had swallowed poison and was going to die soon. I looked at his mother, asked if everything was alright with him, and she confirmed my suspicion that he was lying. Theatrics.

And then it hit me; the implications were significant. The lies, the imagination, the attachment to feel compelled to interact, the lack of exposure, the need to feel wanted. Matthew didn't have any brothers or sisters. He was raised by both his mother and grandmother. They let him go in and out of the house as he pleased. He had no guidance, at least not any constructive guidance. His mother and her lies; they indicated a trend. Somewhere, Matthew learned how to fabricate wild stories to draw attention to himself; to be less insignificant to his mom. He had already lost his dad, who was nowhere to be found. Matthew's emotions of loneliness projected outward. One of the key differences between him and his mother was that she had been through life. She had been through enough experiences to know where the border between reality and complete implausibility met. It is only a matter of time before Matthew too realizes how far he can stretch the truth before someone sees through it

Matthew needed the attention his mother and grandmother never gave him. He needed guidance and stability; he needed someone to listen. He may never know proper from improper if he continues to be saturated by the illusion of life his mother and grandmother exposed him to. When I met Matthew, he needed to tell these stories. He needed to play, to experiment, to be exposed to something beyond his current situation. Matthew needed to break the cycle that his mom and his surroundings had supported.

I tell this story because it frightens me. It scares me to see that at twelve, what a person's future will most probably extrapolate to because of their surroundings. And it hurts to see that a child can pick up so many behaviors, embed them into their psyche, and live their life from there. Will he ever know how detrimental his past has been to his future life? Will his parents know? How many of us are there that are blinded by the problems of our current life that we have missed understanding the importance of our past? How many of us are like Matthew? There is always the chance of Matthew extending himself beyond his past experiences. My point is that Matthew has not been treated right. That will stifle him in the future. It will make it much more difficult to break a cycle that has become his personality. Interacting with the world will become a more challenging feat, since his exposure to relationships has been concentrated to learning from his mother and grandmother. It will make it that much more difficult to create his own future instead of perpetuating his mother's challenges. And this is something that many of us face, continuing to live out the problems of our past without knowing it.

We need to question what we've been through. We need to question the aspects of our personalities that we don't assign meaning to. In order to live happier lives, we have to acknowledge and assess the roles that our individual histories play on them. After that last day of seeing Matthew, I began to visit the community garden more frequently. It was during the summer as the temperature warmed up that I eyed the blue tent that Matthew said chickens were in. I chuckled, reminiscing on such a wild experience over the past year.

Then the wind blew the tent back. There were chickens.

ABOUT THE AUTHOR

(704) 299-9873

www.ingramcontent.com/pod-product-compliance
Lightning Source LLC
Chambersburg PA
CBHW050824160426
43192CB00010B/1886